How to
Survive
the '80s

How to Survive the '80s

By
Lewis R. Walton and
Herbert E. Douglass

PACIFIC PRESS
PUBLISHING ASSOCIATION
Mountain View, California
Oshawa, Ontario

Contents

WELCOME to a journey into the future.

The positive concepts you are about to read
   have already helped millions of people
   find answers that work.

Simply by following the formula for survival
   revealed here, you can
        live confidently
        welcome challenge
        turn tragedy into a constructive experience
        inspire others to face the future unafraid

And you will get a fascinating glimpse
   of the tomorrow everyone is
   wondering about.

Tomorrow Is Not
for the Weak

If you are like millions of other alert people, you
have come to the conclusion that your future is being
shaped by forces you cannot even clearly identify,
much less control. Storm flags are flying everywhere.
Like the majority of your neighbors, you probably believe that the future could be a time of real trouble.

For one thing, the economy has played strange
tricks on you. Unless you are a fortunate exception,
your financial goals are drifting hopelessly out of
reach. There simply is no surplus anymore. Even the
credit system, which once handed you tomorrow's
treats today, has turned snappish, like a family dog
grown unpredictable in its old age. Almost without notice, you have switched from *getting ahead* to merely
surviving.

You probably worry about how the future will treat
your children or grandchildren, about the quality of
their education and the value system they are likely to
adopt. At times you may feel a twinge of fear as you
put them on a school bus or send them on an errand;
for you know that this year many such children, on just
such errands, will not return.

Something is happening to the delicate machinery
we call civilization. It still operates, but deep in the
gears we hear strange sounds, as if the machine itself

were breaking up. In America's overcrowded court-rooms people routinely ask the government to inter-vene in minor problems that would have been solved informally a few years ago. In some third-world coun-tries, millions of starving people drift aimlessly, beg-ging for food in the aftermath of revolutions that were supposed to have made the world better.

In rural counties bands of heavily armed men roam over acres of secluded woodland, learning to conduct paramilitary maneuvers. People you would call com-munity pillars—doctors, lawyers, corporate officers—pore over maps, studying population growth and nu-clear fallout patterns, trying to find the last "safe" place on earth. From time to time, they tramp the woods together, firing weapons and eating freeze-dried food, the advance guard of a great host of nervous peo-ple, frightened by the future, who are trying to learn how to meet it.

On a ridge in California's Santa Cruz Mountains, en-veloped by hulking redwoods and sprawling manzanitas, members of Survival on Site (SOS) are nestled in their redwood-and-glass villas, protected by a hydraulically operated steel gate. Engineers, doc-tors, nurses, aerospace scientists, and salesmen, with ages spanning 20-70, have each developed his own ten acres into properties averaging $280,000.

Enjoying life to the fullest now, they anticipate the ravages of hell—anything from a first-class earthquake to a nuclear knockout. On a recent evening they heard a speaker say, "There are dozens of disasters to con-sider. Did you know that California experiences 5000 earthquakes a year? We're due for the Big One. Then there's the possibility of forest fires, floods, race riots, depressions, famine, chemical spills, trucker's strikes, drought, nuclear accidents, nuclear war—" The list went on. The group debated the top twenty disasters and their respective probabilities.

They hope for the best and prepare for the worst. One of the leaders of SOS explained that he doesn't want to do anything foolish: if disaster doesn't come, he won't be worse off; if it does, he will be better off. And one of the worst situations, he believes, is to be so foolish as to depend on city or county facilities should a disaster occur: "There will be hundreds of thousands of people in line ahead of you."

So the group has its gardens, beehives, barns, solar-heated tri-levels, stored dried food, weapons and ammunition (including crossbows), chickens and goats, diesel generators, water pumps, ham radios, and special classes on self-defense.

Meanwhile, renowned scholars warn us of a collapsing freshwater system, an overpopulated planet, and a mounting crisis in key raw materials.

The economy. Society. Energy. Military threat. Something is coming—but what? You see the warning signals, and a familiar thought plagues your mind like an annoying old acquaintance you'd rather not see again: *shouldn't you be doing something?*

You think about getting away from urban risks, about becoming more self-sufficient, and perhaps you casually glance at the rural real-estate section of the Sunday classified ads, wondering how a person goes about making an escape. Escape? To what? Your world is built around a family home, a life-style, a familiar job. You want to act, but you are not ready to take your family on a dramatic leap into the unknown, where the survival challenges might be worse than those from which you ran. So, chances are, you fold the paper and push the thought aside once again, deciding to gamble on better news next week.

In the deeper recesses of your mind, where brews up tomorrow's migraines, you are still not satisfied. Something about your whole life-style seems headed for trouble, and many of your neighbors also sense it. You notice that some are storing food in their garage. Others disappear on weekends, spending time at a "cabin" they've found in the comfortable foothills of the next county. (They are reluctant to say much about it or to give its exact location.) Firearms sales are up at your local sporting-goods stores. Your city library bulges with doomsday books. Private-investment newsletters, proclaiming the wisdom of investing in such items as gold, silver, and powdered peanut butter, are proudly in view on living-room coffee tables or are passed from friend to friend like maps to hidden treasures. Survivalism has become one of the most explosive growth industries of the 1980s. Too many people are concerned. You can no longer rest comfortably doing nothing.

What you are looking for, of course, is a survival plan of your own—preferably one which will not require the outlay of a great deal of money. It will need to be flexible, because the challenges you face could come from any of several directions. It will also need to be practical. You are not in the mood for fine-spun theories; you want commonsense steps that can readily be put into practice. And when you get this mental shopping list all assembled, you may well conclude that it is a tall order

Tall, but not impossible. For the ultimate survival plan has already been written. It is as near as your front door. It is called *nature,* and the lessons it offers could change your whole future. Let us explain.

In researching the topic of survival in the 1980s, we began with the books and literature which this phenomenal new industry has produced. We learned about buying diamonds and building wind machines. We saw pictures of idyllic hideaways in the New England woodlands and read about paramilitary bunkers in the rock-rimmed canyons of central Oregon.

Yet, while some of these ideas make interesting reading, we could not erase from our minds the haunting picture of France in 1939. After World War I, French politicians vowed never again to submit to foreign invasion. From the Vosges Mountains to the Ardennes, earthmoving equipment cut a huge gash in the ground into which went tank traps, concrete, and heavy guns. Whole military cities were buried beneath the soil of Lorraine, a defensive line that seemed virtually impregnable. But therein lay a fatal miscalculation which only the future could expose: France was facing tomorrow's challenges with yesterday's data. The trench-and-machine-gun mentality that had thrown back entire enemy divisions in 1917 was now utterly inadequate for confronting the tractored panzers of 1940. The Nazi invasion simply moved around the northern end of France's mighty Maginot Line the way a boy might step around a fallen log.

Many of the modern survival suggestions we reviewed seemed to contain the same flaws that troubled France. Most of them are highly involved and depend on one's skill in buying and selling high-priced commodities such as gold and silver. Basic to many plans are the building of fixed defense shelters and the accumulation and storing of *things*—all of which may be useful if the future is kind enough to follow the same script used by the "specialist" who designed your particular survival plan!

Some of the plans depend on skill with weapons. That is worrisome; few people are capable of surviving a shoot-out. Besides, most of these ideas are simply too expensive or too impractical for the average person to afford! We were puzzled. There had to be an answer, something which could be used *regardless of a person's wealth or education*.

The answer came into focus one day as we read about a fortress someone had built in the American Northwest—a concrete bunker perched on the side of a rocky mountain, filled with weapons and food. Yet, within a few decades, it will begin to crumble, its foundation split by blades of grass. The concrete will fail; the grass will survive. That gave us the clue for which we were searching!

We started over, determined to look at even the most basic questions in a new light. For the time being we laid aside the survival manuals and newsletters (they would come in handy later, but only after we had sorted out our priorities). Something more basic now intrigued us: does nature itself offer survival techniques that stand even when Maginot Lines fail?

The answer lies ahead of you, in the pages you are about to read. The program you will discover may be different from anything you have ever read. Make no mistake. It will require some special attention on your part and a mind wide open to new ideas. You'll likely find yourself wanting to make changes which may at first seem unusual. But these changes will soon be such a natural part of your life you'll wonder how you ever got along without them.

You'll have to do some studying. Why? Because the future will not be kind to the unprepared. And you'll have to learn how to pick your allies. Tomorrow will be a hazardous place if you intend to go it alone. You'll need help, and you'll need to know where to find it.

But we think the rewards are worth every moment

you will spend. What you are about to discover is a life-style in which survival is not a morbid obsession, but rather a by-product of something even larger—something that could enrich your life today.

Therefore, we are not pessimists. And we don't want you to be pessimists, either. Optimists plan to survive when troubles come; pessimists see only troubles and not positive alternatives, virtually suggesting they would rather be dead.

Nothing is more exciting than the "good life." Travel, hitting the white water in the rapids, reaching the top of your profession, building the dream house and filling it with happy children—all this comes easier, perhaps faster, to the survivalist.

Let's begin with the first step in nature's program for survival. It involves *you*—your ability to handle change, your endurance under stress.

Let's talk about your health. *Tomorrow is not for the weak.*

Begin With Yourself

Try to imagine the worst possible disaster that could strike you and your family. Start with financial failure—bills so catastrophic you have little hope of ever paying them off. Bankruptcy looms. You learn a whole new vocabulary, hastily explained to you by an attorney. Exemptions. Referees. Chapter something-or-other. The terms swim in your mind. Translated, they mean that you are headed for a very different life-style.

Think you have problems? You have only begun. Toss in another blockbuster: loss of all *future* income, so that you have even less hope of ever recovering from your pending bankruptcy. Add the psychological trauma that will scar your spouse and children and the probable disruption of your children's educational plans. Finally, to round things out, include the impact of your own death on your family's well-being.

It is difficult to imagine a more complete and devastating scenario. It contains everything you fear in the future: economic disaster, personal trauma, even death. Neither worldwide depression nor foreign invasion could offer much worse. But if you could know in advance that such dangers were imminent, you would spare no expense or effort to escape. Nothing would be too hard or too expensive if it offered even a small chance of survival.

Suppose, however, that by using nature's survival rules you could achieve the same results, save yourself and your family, and do so absolutely free. Suppose you could actually *lessen* your present monthly cost of living. You would have a secret of such enormous value that your neighbors would pay you almost any price to learn it.

That secret we now share with you. But first some gentle reminders. Tomorrow's challenges will not be for the weak. Make no mistake about it. We are headed for a time of trouble as bad as (and some say worse than) anything human history has seen. Never has the entire world been so pathetically dependent on an interlocking economic-military-political structure so riddled with stress cracks that even experts wonder, from day to day, what keeps it from collapsing.

In a moving and eloquent farewell, President Carter warned the United States (and the world) that the danger of nuclear war is growing and that civilization itself may be committing suicide: "It may be only a matter of time before madness, desperation, greed, or miscalculation lets loose this terrible force."

Friedrich von Hayek, Nobel Prize laureate and world-renowned economist, said in a recent interview: "You have no choice now in the United States. Sooner or later you must go through this very unpleasant process of stopping inflation, thereby producing large-scale unemployment and a great deal of suffering and dissatisfaction."

Financial experts remind us that our enormous borrowing on the future has created an inflationary psychology that few expect ever to be cured. In other words, money itself is going broke, and everyone in the 1980s can see where it may end by merely looking back to the collapse of Germany's economy in the 1920s.

Therefore, because tomorrow's challenges are not for the weak, the first line of defense in your survival plan will be your own health. No survival plan means much without personal health, because tomorrow promises a grim world for the chronically unhealthy person. For one thing, the cost of health care has already gone through the roof, forcing the American federal government to reverse the trend of decades as it cuts back medical assistance to the elderly. Some government health planners go further and are talking quietly about rationing health-care services, eliminating payment for procedures that do not produce results on a "cost-effective" basis. In simple terms, they are saying that if your disease has, say, a 20 percent cure rate, government planners in the years ahead may determine that your disease is statistically not worth treating, at least not with federal money.

In other words, in the days ahead you will have to have everything working in your favor, beginning with your health. Not only to avoid the high costs of health care, but also to find the stamina for survival in tough times.

Earlier we suggested that you think about an assortment of challenges in which you might face financial disaster, family disruption, a shattered future, and the risk of death. What we described is not some storybook exaggeration, too horrible to happen to you. It *does* happen—a million times a year in the United States alone. It's called *cardiovascular disease*.

Try another scenario. Take the same troubles we just described and modify them. Instead of a sudden disruption, think of a slow, lingering death for you or for a family member, probably accompanied by a great deal of pain. No, we're not talking about some form of doomsday radiation sickness; this danger is much more immediate. It's called *cancer;* and, in the United States alone, it kills some 430,000 people annually—one person every seventy-three seconds! Directly and indirectly, it will cost more than thirty billion dollars—an incredible waste dumped on an already sagging economy.

Heart disease and cancer—only two examples. We could give many more. But they are sufficient to illustrate the everyday challenges you face even before your long-term survival plan gets off the ground. Of all Americans who will die this year, three out of four will succumb to one of these two diseases. That is 1,400,000 people—more Americans lost each year than were killed in every war from the American Revolution to Vietnam put together! In other words, you have less-than-battlefield odds of escaping these two killers.

Now here is the good news. Science already knows how to cut the risk of death from heart attack by *at least 50 percent*. Regarding cancer, responsible researchers now are saying that the overall risk of death from cancer could be cut by *80 percent*, simply by using some commonsense ideas we already know— ideas anyone can put into practice. That means we could probably prevent or postpone more than 800,000 deaths right now, using *present* knowledge. For survivalists, that is an awesome beginning—tremendous inside information.

By now a question may be brewing: if all this is so well known, why haven't we simply eradicated these diseases? With heart disease, perhaps, we have begun to do that—just barely. Death rates from heart attacks are on the decrease, simply because more and more people are learning what you are about to learn and are putting these ideas into practice. But despite some progress, heart disease still needlessly claims a million lives in the United States annually. And cancer rates remain high. All because most people either don't know what you are going to learn or are unwilling to use the bit of self-discipline it takes to put these ideas into daily use. In the end (sooner than any victim thinks) many will pay a very high price for their negligence. You need not.

Let's begin then, with the $64 billion question: How is it done?

A few years ago an eminent researcher, Dr. Lester Breslow*, dean of the School of Public Health at UCLA, startled the scientific community with the statement that Americans could add eleven extra years to their lives by following seven commonsense health habits. Here they are:

Don't smoke.

Use little or no alcohol.

Start the day with a good breakfast.

Avoid eating between meals.

Sleep seven to eight hours each night.

Engage in frequent, regular exercise.

Maintain ideal weight and avoid overweight.

Too simple a plan to take seriously? Take a look at the data on which Dr. Breslow and his research team based those conclusions. For nine years they studied a population group, correlating health habits with death rates. If an American man routinely broke just one of those seven rules—a regular healthful breakfast, for example—his survival probability after just nine years dropped by 40 percent!

After nine years a smoker's risk of dying increased

* See Appendix A.1

by almost 70 percent. Heavy drinkers increased their risk by 36 to 46 percent. And men who engaged in the all-American pastime of between-meal snacks dropped their nine-year survival probability by 20 percent! Little rules—enormous consequences.

Perhaps the most startling feature of Dr. Breslow's study was that following his suggested rules of health does not require multimillion dollar technology. *They are available to everyone, regardless of education or income*. At least two of them—the restrictions on smoking and drinking—will actually save you money! And another one, which we will cover shortly, could cut your food costs by up to 40 percent each month.

Like most people, we had heard about these simple rules that promise such spectacular results. And we wanted to know more about how they work and about how to put them into practice. It was time, we decided, to consult one of the best experts we could find on the subject.

In operation all across North America, the Pacific, and Australasia is a highly successful (and much-imitated) coronary-risk screening program called Heartbeat. Perhaps you have gone through a Heartbeat evaluation in your hometown. Participants have their blood analyzed for risk factors related to heart disease and several other major diseases. They also complete a detailed life-style and health-history analysis which give the reviewing doctor a good view of their personal health and hereditary risks. This analysis, together with their weight, blood-chemistry studies, and blood pressure, is used to produce a very helpful profile of their potential risks.

But the program does not stop with mere analysis. It also tells people how to overcome those risks through effective follow-up programs, such as weight control, low-cholesterol cooking, blood pressure clinics, stop-smoking programs, and cancer-risk-reduction seminars. It is a practical program geared not only to identifying problems but to solving them. Looking for just that sort of practical approach to health, we decided to go straight to Dr. John Scharffenberg, the originator of the Heartbeat program—a physician and Harvard-trained health educator. Slim and energetic, he works at a university-affiliated hospital in central California where he heads one of the most innovative community health-education programs in America today. Our research team joined him in a Chinese restaurant one afternoon, and while he ordered a zero-cholesterol dinner in fluent Mandarin, we prepared to learn how we can harness health principles for better overall survival.

Scharffenberg plunged into his topic. "If I were going to write about survival in the 1980s, of course I'd start with health. Why? Because right now we're needlessly losing over 800,000 lives each year—worse than any disaster you can imagine short of nuclear war. The tragedy is that we already know how to save many of those lives by using commonsense rules.

"Let me explain how we in the scientific community came to the conclusion that heart disease, cancer, and other major diseases are controllable *now*. A number of years ago researchers decided to compare Americans with people in countries where heart-attack death rates are low. American men were compared with Japanese men; the Americans had a heart-attack mortality rate many times greater than the Japanese, who live mainly on foods low in cholesterol and saturated fat. Some, however, feared that the conclusions might have inaccuracies because of the genetic and other differences between Americans and Japanese.

"What we really needed was to find a group of Americans who have low heart-disease death rates and compare them with other Americans who have the usual high risk. That would eliminate the variables which left some scientists skeptical about the international studies.

"The problem, of course, was finding *any* group of Americans low in heart-disease risk. But about ten years ago a team of university researchers did so at Loma Linda University, in Loma Linda, California. They decided to study a sizable group* of men and women whose diet and life-style is strikingly similar to the one suggested by Dr. Breslow's famous seven rules of health. In addition, this group emphasizes a low intake of cholesterol and saturated fat. The study went on for several years, comparing their disease rates with those of the general population, and, in 1979, the results were ready for publication.

"Although we had expected to see some differences, we were totally unprepared for how spectacular the differences turned out to be. The men in this group who carefully follow their dietary and health guidelines have only 12 percent of the average death rate from heart attack! Their advantage is over eightfold! But that is just the beginning. In nearly every category of major cancer they also enjoy a significantly reduced risk of death. Other studies showed lower average blood pressure. Their risk of death from stroke and diabetes was only about half that of the average American, and their death rate from peptic ulcer was just 42 percent of the average expectancy. Dr. Breslow's simple rules of health can produce some fantastic, across-the-board benefits."

One of those benefits, we discovered, is *six extra*

* See Appendix A.2

years of life expectancy. The studies indicate that the average California male in the control group, age 35-64, can expect to live 6.2 years longer than his California counterpart. Obviously, a program of health based on easy-to-apply principles is worth exploring.

Now let's talk about how to do it. We'll start with Breslow's seven rules and add two or three more disclosed by the university-researched health study Scharffenberg referred to. We'll have an easy-to-follow program in which you, too, can lessen your risk of disease, increase your overall survival quotient, and perhaps even add a half-dozen years to your life—while lowering your monthly expenses!

1. WHAT TO DO ABOUT SMOKING

If you are a nonsmoker, your risk of lung cancer is up to 80 percent less than that of your smoking neighbor. While you're thinking about that, consider the other advantages you enjoy: a much lower risk of death from mouth, throat, and bladder cancers. Reduced danger of getting the terrible disability called emphysema, in which the lungs cease to function properly, making every breath hard work. Better physical endurance and night vision. Lowered risk of heart disease and avoidance of such bizarre problems as Raynaud's disease—a condition in which the fingertips become blue and very painful because tobacco has constricted the blood vessels so much that the fingers do not get a sufficient blood supply.

If you are a smoker, plan to quit. You'll rediscover the joy of smelling fresh morning air, of actually tasting your food. And if you're worried about gaining weight after quitting tobacco, keep reading—we have a weight-control program coming up in just a few pages that will work for you.

If you have been smoking for very long, quitting may not be easy. We know that. In fact, you may have discovered already that you need help. Many commercial programs are available to help you, some of them quite expensive. If you'd rather save money and get lasting help at the same time, we have discovered that a Five-Day Plan to Stop Smoking is available in most communities. Designed by a doctor-minister team who wanted to do something to help their community, it now is conducted all over America, Australia, Canada, and in many other countries. More than a million persons have already reported great success.

If you cannot get to such a program, here are some hints to help you through the first few days:

a. *Believe you can do it*. The only time you can't change is when you're dead—and that's the hazard you want to avoid. Believe in yourself. If you have a religious faith, plan to use it now more than you have used it for years. Remind yourself that over thirty million people, just in America, have quit. There is no reason why you cannot. Some find quitting easier than others do. Regardless, whether easy or hard, start saying, "I choose not to smoke."

b. *Use water*—one of nature's most powerful and inexpensive "drugs." Think for a moment. Your whole system is saturated with nicotine. Your first priority is to get that drug leached out of your body as soon as possible, and water is the ideal agent to do just that. Drink six or even eight glasses daily *between meals*, and, if you have to, keep a record of your water intake.

Don't drink coffee. The famous Russian psychologist Pavlov once called coffee "bad-habit glue" because it makes it harder for you to quit. (Sit down for a cup of coffee and what is the first thing you'll be reaching for?) For the same reason, don't drink beer, wine, or hard liquor. At this point you need to give your willpower every advantage; the last thing it needs is a deadening blow from alcohol.

Next, use water on the outside of your body. This is the one time in your life when you deserve every legitimate luxury. Bathe or shower often to relieve the distressing symptoms of nicotine withdrawal. (Here is a side benefit: it's hard to smoke in the shower!) Start with pleasantly warm water, and cool your shower by degrees until you can take it cold. Try alternating three minutes of hot with thirty seconds of cold water. Blood vessels which have grown sluggish because of nicotine will perk up much more quickly if you try this technique. A sauna or steam bath may also provide helpful relaxation, but avoid the extremes of temperature.

c. *Get plenty of rest.* Be sure you have eight hours of sleep each night during the first week or so. Retire earlier than usual. Your willpower needs the help of restful sleep.

d. *After meals, get up at once.* If you sit around, you'll be reaching for a cigarette out of habit. Take a brisk walk in the open air where the stale smell of last week's cigarettes will not call out to you from the drapes and carpet.

Play a round of golf or go to a hobby shop. Do anything to keep your mind occupied. And breathe deeply. The frontal lobes of the brain, where your willpower resides, are especially dependent on oxygen.

e. *Avoid heavily spiced foods, gravies, fried food, and rich desserts.* You have probably become very accustomed to all of these. Why? Because, if you are a typical smoker, tobacco has deadened your taste buds, thus forcing you to use more and more seasonings in order to enjoy your food. After you stop smoking and your taste buds return to normal, you won't need highly spiced or rich foods. Many people have remarked that a highly seasoned rare steak gives them a strong craving for tobacco. Avoid the sort of food which makes your work harder.

f. *But eat these foods: fresh fruit, vegetables, whole-grain products.* If you like oriental food, this is the time to eat it. Cut down your intake of salt. Taste your food before reaching for the salt shaker (many people don't), and educate your taste toward less salt. With less salt, your weight may be easier to control, and your blood pressure certainly will be. If you like, take some extra B vitamins, either as supplements or in the natural form. (Brewers' yeast is an excellent natural source of B vitamins.)

2. AVOID ALCOHOL

In Dr. Breslow's study, those who regularly had four or more drinks in a row suffered a 36-percent increase in the risk of death over the nine-year period of the study. Alcohol is associated with head and neck cancers. When combined with smoking, it increases the risk of oral cancer dramatically. Alcohol can produce acute and sometimes fatal bouts of pancreatitis. It is associated with half of our fatal traffic accidents. And it is enormously expensive—in initial cost, lost productivity, and in the decline of personal values.

The Loma Linda University health study we mentioned earlier turned up some interesting facts regarding alcohol and tobacco. Rather than playing the game of "moderation" with these drugs, the control group avoided them totally, mindful of the fact that alcohol turns one of every ten "moderate" users into an alcoholic. In the Loma Linda study, researchers analyzed the health benefits to a group of people who neither smoke nor drink. Here are the results, showing how Loma Linda's control group enjoyed a lower risk of those diseases related to smoking and drinking:

Control Group Risk of Death

(Control group's rate of contracting disease compared to the general population's disease contracting rate—the general population's rate being considered 100%)

All Cancer	59%
Heart disease	55%
Diabetes	55%
Stroke	53%
Peptic ulcer	42%
Emphysema	32%
Suicide	31%
Lung cancer	20%

3. A GOOD BREAKFAST

A surprising number of people have developed a strange pattern of eating that affects their productivity, their risk of disease, and the way they feel. Let's follow the dietary habits of a typical, middle-aged male.

Breakfast time arrives, and—if he would admit it to himself—he is simply in no condition to face food. His last major act of the previous evening was to eat a huge, heavy, high-fat meal before collapsing in front of the television. All night his overworked digestive system has been trying to process too much of the wrong kind of food, taken at the one time of day when he didn't need to eat very much. Now, feeling the morning blahs, he passes the breakfast table with the excuse that he "doesn't have time" for more than a doughnut and a cup of coffee. With that unpromising beginning, he heads for work.

Toward midmorning, last night's meal has finally worn off. Now he really begins to feel the lack of a good breakfast. At the ten o'clock coffee break he continues his series of unfortunate food encounters—usually in the form of some concentrated sweet (devoid of the vitamin B_1 needed to metabolize sugar) together with another cup or two of coffee. His bloodstream gets a quick jolt of empty calories, and the desire for a proper lunch drops considerably.

Lunch is often a meal in which the main components are fried foods or meat (which tend to raise blood-cholesterol levels), and more caffeine—either in coffee or a cola drink. By midafternoon, hunger once again creeps up, demanding to be satisfied by a snack at coffee time.

At this point, his body has been going for several hours on the most meager nourishment. Chronic hunger is setting in. Often, the lack of essential vitamins begins to manifest itself in the form of jumpy nerves, an irritable temper, and energy fadeout. His body is doing its best but is fighting a losing battle. Ignoring the reason for his distress, he complains about job tension—and may wonder why he doesn't enjoy career advancement. At 5 he heads home to face the day's grand finale—too much of the wrong kind of food, at the worst time of day!

Late in the day, *long after the body needs* all that excess nourishment, he sits down to a dinner table laden with saturated fat, cholesterol, and excess sugar—a combination that goes to work manufacturing a condition called heart disease.

After the meal, he finds his comfortable chair in the family room to be entertained by a phosphorescent box. Exercise—the one item that might have helped him—vanishes into the night. The next morning he awakens, wondering why he feels so rotten—and the whole, destructive cycle repeats itself.

Now let's rewrite that script, using Breslow's rules and some ideas from the university health study. This time our hypothetical friend is a middle-aged American male who follows Breslow's first rule of always eating a good breakfast. In so doing he enjoys a 40 percent higher survival rate than his neighbor who grabs the doughnut and coffee—or less. He awakens early, refreshed by a good night's sleep, and is enormously hungry. Why? Because his digestive tract has not been working all night trying to process an almost indigestible mass of saturated fat, cholesterol, sugar, and too-much-of-everything.

What did our friend eat for supper? A light meal composed predominantly of fruits, or a vegetable salad—foods which digest rapidly because there is little fat to slow digestion and plenty of fiber to speed it up. When a person eats a heavy, high-fat meal just before retiring, the digestive process is sluggish.

The first morning you awaken after following this light-supper routine, you'll know that something is already better about your life-style. You'll probably awaken early because you have slept better. Take advantage of that! You already have an hour or two on your competition!

If you really want to treat your body right, start the morning with exercise—and you don't necessarily have to jog. Actually, for most people, a fast walk is safer and probably as beneficial as jogging.

After your exercise, you're ready for the next step in facing the day. Take a hot shower, and then turn up the cold. The first time you do this you may think that survival isn't worth the effort, but give it a try. (Careful about this if you have known heart disease or any other condition which might respond poorly to sudden temperature stresses. Always ask your physician if in doubt.) When you emerge from this routine you will have little doubt about your ability to handle anything the day throws at you.

Why is a simple shower so important? A hot-and-cold shower in the morning gives your vascular system a real workout. First, the warm water draws blood to the surface, expanding the capillaries in your skin. Then the quick, cold shower constricts these surface vessels and forces the blood back into the deeper tissues. Your vessels thus get a double workout. Your circulation is improved, and you have all the stimulation you need to face the morning—without the disadvantages of coffee nerves.

Now a second reason why you should shower this way: exposure to the brief stress of cold water puts your body's immunity mechanism in a fighting mood. Your white-blood-cell count goes up, meaning you can more effectively fight off disease-causing germs. Using this technique, together with a low-sugar diet, you may go years without ever catching a common cold! This is a surprisingly powerful means of disease prevention. Try it.

By this time you will have fork and spoon eagerly in hand. You will not be merely hungry, you may well be ravenous! You'll face the first meal of the day with new gusto.

If you enjoy eating—if the sight of food rings pleasant melodies—breakfast is the one time of day you can really enjoy yourself. After all, you have a whole day in which to work off the calories, and if you approach your job the way most people do who follow this routine, you'll need them. (Sooner or later your boss will notice, and you'll find that this program has some nice effects on career advancement.)

We'll talk more about diet later, with hints on specific foods that do you the most good, so we'll not say anything more about breakfast right now except *enjoy it*. You earned it!

If you eat a proper breakfast, ten o'clock should find you very uninterested in snacking. If so, good. Between-meal snacks caused a 20 percent mortality increase for the men in Dr. Breslow's study. The doughnut you eat at coffee break will only add pounds hard to get rid of. Such snacks also urge you back toward old habits of eating the wrong things at the wrong times—and soon you'll be right back where you started, feeling awful and wondering why.

While you're at it, why not think about eliminating coffee as well? Scientists are becoming alarmed over the growing list of dangers posed by caffeine. High blood pressure. Ulcers. Possibly bladder and pancreatic cancer. Even birth defects, which seem statistically related to a mother's intake of coffee during pregnancy.

Then, too, if you are fighting other old habits such as smoking or between-meal snacking, you will find your task much harder if you continue the coffee habit—with which they are often associated. Remember Pavlov's "bad-habit glue."

Finally, why stimulate your system chemically? A good night's rest and a cold shower at the start of the day provide plenty of stimulation without any unpleasant side effects. When you do get tired, your system deserves the luxury of a little rest rather than a chemical jolt. (Here's a hint: during coffee breaks, go outside and walk for ten minutes. You'll return to work relaxed and refreshed.)

You are now well on your way toward a truly successful day. You have had a good breakfast, you have avoided unnecessary foods at midmorning, and now lunchtime approaches. If you had the sort of breakfast we will recommend in a few pages, you'll probably find that noontime doesn't find you terribly hungry. That means that the system is working for you. If you can delay your lunch an hour or two, eating at the very end of the noon hour or even later, you'll find that you will reap a lot of benefits. You won't have a long line ahead of you in restaurants, and your fellow workers might appreciate someone who is willing to stagger the lunch-hour schedule with them. Furthermore, your boss may find it very helpful to have someone around when everyone else is away. And by eating a later lunch in the afternoon, you'll forestall the urge to eat a big meal when you get home.

With your later lunch hour, the afternoon will sail by; it will, after all, be an hour or two shorter. Chances are you will return home feeling like you've worked a seven-hour day, and you'll have energy to spare for enjoying the part of the day that truly belongs to you—the time for family, friends and hobbies.

Now comes suppertime. If you ate properly at lunch, you may not feel the need of an evening meal—and pounds will melt off before you know what is happening. If you eat light, easily digested food, your digestive tract will reward you with another good night's sleep, your heart will thank you in extra years of service, and you may notice, after a short time, that your mental alertness has improved.

All this because you began the day with a good breakfast. A simple rule—a profound, far-reaching change that touches every part of your day, adds years to your life, and just possibly offers you job advancement!

4. EATING BETWEEN MEALS

One of the first rules we teach our children is also one of the first rules we ourselves break—eating between meals. We are literally assaulted with a multibillion-dollar array of "convenience" foods, which are usually either high in salt or sugar. For many people, a high salt intake is associated with high blood pressure.

Many of these snack foods are also high in saturated fat, which causes the body to produce more cholesterol. What, by the way, is saturated fat? Without getting overly technical, it is a form of fat in which hydrogen atoms are hooked onto every available space in the fat molecule, producing a substance which is often solid at room temperature. Research suggests that it causes a buildup of cholesterol in the coronary arteries. In excess, saturated fat causes havoc in the human vascular system. We get most of our saturated fats from animal products such as butterfat and meat, together with a few highly saturated vegetable oils such as coconut, palm, and cottonseed oils. Learn to read labels, and avoid products with shortenings such as lard, beef fat, or the vegetable oils we just listed—especially if they are "hydrogenated."

Unfortunately, most of the foods we are accustomed to eating between meals have all these ingredients. That is bad enough, but to make things worse, we eat this junk food at the worst possible time. The digestive tract is still trying to handle what we ate two hours before; now it must work again, with no hope of rest. Blood-sugar levels shoot up. Appetite is depressed at *regular* mealtimes. And the sweet or salty junk food we eat has few vitamins or fiber to offset its ill effects. Small wonder that men who regularly ate between meals suffered a 20 percent mortality increase.

5. ADEQUATE REST

In Dr. Breslow's study, men who regularly slept less than six hours a night had a 36 percent greater death rate than men who slept seven to eight hours.

For those who have trouble sleeping soundly, remember what we said earlier about diet, heavy suppers, and sleep. The more we eat in the evening, the less soundly we are apt to sleep. And a daily exercise program is one of nature's best sleeping pills.

Then there's worry. Many people allow anxiety to intrude into their sleeping hours. We all have discovered that no problem looks as bad in daylight as it does at 3:00 a.m. If you have faith in God, here is the time to put it into practice. If you don't yet have such faith, think seriously about finding it. The future will be a terribly lonely and scary place for those who do not have some deep belief in divine help.

6. REGULAR EXERCISE

In America, heart-attack death rates have already started down. Not a lot, but enough to encourage doctors who work in public health. Dr. Scharffenberg attributes this trend to a new concern about life-style—less smoking, better blood pressure control, less saturated fat, better exercise habits. If you eat properly and exercise, it is difficult to get in trouble with your heart.

For that matter, the rules often work well even if you are already in trouble with your heart. Dr. Scharffenberg, an advisory board member for Dr. Nathan Pritikin's famed Longevity Research Institute, explained how hundreds of extremely ill heart patients have gone through the Pritikin program of low-fat food and lots of daily exercise. "One lady had such severe angina that she couldn't walk across the room without taking nitroglycerine," he commented. "After one month of eating properly and carefully increasing her exercise, she could walk miles a day without pain. I invited her to talk to a hundred people in one of my health-education programs, and you should have seen the astonished audience. Here was a lady who had been totally disabled by heart disease but who was now free from pain—through a simple program of diet and exercise anyone could use at home!''

What was her exercise secret? Walking—the best universal exercise you can possibly get.

A fast walk works the whole body evenly, avoids the problems such as arthritic flareups some joggers experience, and gives you time to think about the day in a calm, positive way.

To get maximum benefit, be sure you walk at *least* twenty minutes without stopping. For most beginners this will be a little over a mile. Start at the pace which seems most comfortable for you, gradually working up to the point where you are actually striding. As you do, the distance you walk in twenty minutes will gradually lengthen.

The object is to get your pulse rate up to a target level which is computed in a simple way to insure your safety. Take the number 200 and subtract from that number your own age. Then, to be extra safe, knock off another 10 percent from that figure. Each time you exercise you should try to get your pulse up to (but not over) that number.

Let's illustrate. Suppose you are fifty years old. Subtract fifty from 200, and you are left with 150. Now subtract 10 percent of 150 (15), and you have 135. That rate—135 heartbeats per minute—is what you should reach to enjoy maximum benefit from your exercise if you are fifty years old. Naturally, see your doctor before trying any new program if you have had heart trouble or if you have risk factors related to it. (If you are on a medication such as Inderal, this target-pulse-rate technique won't work.)

Why twenty minutes without stopping? Because scientists have determined that it takes at least that long for exercise to benefit your heart and lungs. Thirty minutes every day would be even better.

What will this exercise program cost you? Nothing—except, perhaps, an inexpensive pair of walking shoes. Obviously, a half hour a day is worth it.

7. FINDING YOUR IDEAL WEIGHT

Weight control can be much, much easier than you may have thought. And you need not go to expensive clinics or have your teeth wired shut. We are going to give you an absolutely surefire weight-control program in a few simple steps, which you can follow easily and which will cost you nothing. (Your food bill may even decrease!)

These steps are progressive; some people find they lose weight nicely by merely following steps one and two. Others have to include more steps in order to lose weight. Simply follow the program as far as you need to in order to get the weight loss you wish.

Eat a good breakfast. We've already focused on this first rule in weight reduction. When we were discussing the benefits of a good breakfast, you probably didn't realize that it has the added benefit of weight reduction. But think it through, and you'll see how a good breakfast can be one of your best allies in shedding pounds: it helps keep you away from midmorning snacks so high in empty calories; it allows you to eat heartily when you still have the whole day to burn off the calories; and it establishes a pattern which leads you away from the heavy, weight-producing meals most people eat at the end of the day. If you enjoy eating, then do it in the morning. And discipline yourself rigidly the rest of the day.

Skip the snacks. This rule, together with the one we just suggested, may be all you need to lose weight. Take a look at the chart below, and you'll see how many calories sneak through in typical snacks:

Calories in Snack Foods

Cheddar cheese, 1 ounce	115
Chocolate milkshake, 11 ounces	355
Fruit-flavored yogurt, 8 ounces	230
Candy, 1 ounce	115
Milk chocolate candy, 1 ounce	145
Potato chips, 10 pieces	115
Peanuts, one-quarter cup (roasted in oil)	210
Cola beverage, 12 fluid ounces	145
Lemonade, 1 cup	105
Coffee cake, 1 serving	230
Chocolate chip cookies, 4 cookies	205

A suggestion: if you've formed the habit of between-meal snacks, the first few days will be difficult. Your body has grown accustomed to these surges of blood sugar and has developed the habit of giving you a midmorning or midafternoon jolt of insulin. The lack of a snack at the usual time will temporarily depress your blood sugar, giving you a *false* feeling of hunger which may be intense. Fool yourself. Drink a glass or two of cold water to give your stomach the sensation of fullness, and then get busy doing something that will take your mind off food. In a few days your body chemistry will readjust, and you'll find self-restraint much easier.

If you're accustomed to between-meal eating at certain times or in certain locations, avoid activities associated with eating at those times. Give yourself every tactical advantage.

Remove empty and refined calories. Many people find that they want a more aggressive weight-reduction program, and so they move on to this third step. By reducing your intake of nutrition-empty and refined calories you'll find that pounds come off much more quickly.

But how do you do this?

1. Eliminate or drastically reduce your use of all visible fats such as shortening, salad oil, and margarine. Avoid fried foods. Try making your hash-browns in a teflon-lined fry pan without oil. Bake or broil, wherever possible, instead of frying. Use fewer greasy spreads on your bread and rolls.

2. Eliminate or greatly reduce your use of the refined sugar contained in the typical dessert—sweet rolls, ice cream, candy—you know the list as well as we do. Sugar has a paralyzing effect on the white blood cells—one of the body's major defenses against disease. When laboratory animals are given sugar in an amount equivalent to that of a human eating only six teaspoons, their ability to fight disease drops by 25 percent. It also makes some people irritable!

How can you get six teaspoons of sugar? By drinking just one regular-sized cola drink! Twelve teaspoons of sugar reduce disease resistance by 60 percent. Twenty-four teaspoons virtually destroy the ability to fight off disease, reducing it by a catastrophic 92 percent. In the average banana split, you get twenty-five teaspoons! Perhaps that helps to explain why annoying colds and sore throats so often seem to follow overindulgence in sweets. Note the chart on the next page:

Sources of Sugar

	Teaspoons of sugar
Soft drinks, 12 ounce bottle	7
Chocolate cake, average piece	10
Fig Newtons, each	5
Glazed doughnut	6
Fudge square, 1 ounce	4.5
Ice-cream cone	3.5
Milkshake, 10 ounce	5
Strawberry jam, 1 tablespoon	4
Berry pie, one slice	10
Banana split	25

When sugar is combined with fat—and ice cream is a good example—you not only reduce your germ-fighting ability, but you also introduce the raw materials for heart disease. Many scientists think that sugar causes a buildup of fats in the bloodstream, which also increases one's risk of heart disease—particularly in women past the menopause. Sugar also robs the system of vitamins essential for healthy nerve and brain function.

The solution? Learn to enjoy naturally sweet foods such as fruit. While reducing your sugar intake, you'll be getting dietary fiber, which helps to carry off excess cholesterol and to slow down the rate of sugar absorption.

3. Use unrefined products such as whole-grain breads, brown rice, and whole-grain cereals such as granola—a mix of dried fruit and several grains. If you prefer a warm cereal, use oatmeal or some other whole-grain cooked cereal in the morning rather than dry cereal—many of which list sugar as the second ingredient. (Some list it *first;* some even have a sugar content as high as 60 percent!)

Why whole grains? Because more fiber provides many beneficial effects and because the refining process almost always increases the calories you take in. A simple rule to follow is to get your food in as nearly the natural state as possible. That means before commercial food processors have had a chance to mill out essential vitamins, minerals, and trace elements. Refined foods usually have concentrated calories, which is the one thing you don't need right now.

4. Eliminate alcohol. It is high in calories and will depress your willpower.

5. Avoid coffee too, which is often accompanied by high-calorie snacks. Remember that coffee is "bad-habit glue" that makes breaking other old habits more difficult.

Drastically reduce your intake of animal fats. Still want to lose weight more rapidly? Then start cutting down on animal products. They are usually high in saturated fats.

Eat a light supper, or none at all. If you want to put pounds on fast, eat a heavy supper each night and then go to bed. Lots of calories and no exercise equals plenty of pounds—a nearly foolproof system for gaining weight and increasing one's risk of heart disease.

Well, there you have it—five simple steps to find and maintain your ideal weight. You will have a lower risk of diabetes, high blood pressure, even arthritis pain. If you are a woman, your risk of breast and uterine cancer will drop sharply.

We have also briefly studied Dr. Breslow's seven rules for adding many years to your life: don't smoke, curtail alcohol, eat a good breakfast, avoid eating between meals, get adequate sleep, exercise regularly, and maintain ideal weight. These guidelines provide a foundation for good health and personal preparedness on which your whole survival plan can rest securely. They are so simple you can begin today. And they may save you money.

But we are not through. We promised to give you some additional ideas for *avoiding* disease that were discovered in that university research project we mentioned earlier. One of the most exciting discoveries in recent medical research is the fact that the same program that reduces your risk of heart disease also seems to reduce your risk of cancer. Take a look at the graphs on page 43 that show the low death rates from heart disease and cancer enjoyed by the university control group.

When members of this group were studied to discover what makes this startling difference in death rates, researchers discovered that their diet was relatively low in saturated fat, such as is usually found in animal products. The following comparison shows the saturated fat content of many foods. Notice which are at the head of the list.

Percentage of Saturated Fat in Foods

Percentage of Fat Which Is Saturated

Whole milk (1 cup), butter (1 tablespoon)	56
Beef (3 ounces)	50
Pork chop (3.5 ounces)	38
Egg (large)	33
Chicken, fryer (3.2 ounces)	32
Soft margarine (1 tablespoon)	18
Olive oil (1 tablespoon)	11
Corn oil (1 tablespoon)	10

The involvement of meat with heart disease has

CORONARY DEATH RATE FOR CONTROL GROUP COMPARED WITH THE GENERAL POPULATION

Control Group Death Rate

General Population = 100%

% Fewer Deaths Expected Compared to General Population Death Rate

Total vegetarians 14%

(86% less)

Vegetarians who use milk and eggs 39%

(61% less)

Control group who eat meat 56%

(44% less)

CANCER DEATH RATE FOR CONTROL GROUP COMPARED WITH THE GENERAL POPULATION

Control Group

General Population = 100%

% Fewer Deaths Expected Compared to General Population Death Rate

Digestive Tract Cancer 65%

(35% less)

Leukemia 62%

(38% less)

Ovarian Cancer 61%

(39% less)

Uterine Cancer 54%

(46% less)

Bladder Cancer 28%

(72% less)

Lung Cancer 20%

(80% less)

Mouth and Throat Cancer 5%

(95% less)

been suspected for some time. In 1977, the United States Senate Select Committee on Nutrition and Human Needs issued a report urging Americans to eat less meat and to use, instead, high-quality vegetable proteins. The famed Pritikin diet is extremely low in meat and other animal products. More and more scientists are becoming convinced that meat, with its high levels of saturated fats, is responsible for some of our worst diseases.

First on their list is heart disease, because saturated fat in meat causes the body to produce excess cholesterol. But that is only the beginning. Meat has none of the plant fiber necessary to stimulate prompt, healthy digestion and elimination. The food moves sluggishly through the bowel. Without fiber, harmful substances have a longer time in which to act on the body. Cholesterol, which might have been carried off by fiber, instead is reabsorbed into the bloodstream, where it slowly builds up on the lining of the arteries. Thus one problem compounds another—both largely caused by meat in the diet.

Next, researchers have strong reasons to suspect meat's involvement in colon cancer. They have discovered that meat-eating tends to stimulate the body's production of certain chemicals known to cause colon cancer in laboratory animals. Furthermore, because the lack of fiber in meat causes the digestive process to slow down, these harmful chemicals have 250 percent more time to attack the vulnerable lining of the bowels.

In America, colon cancer is the greatest cancer killer after lung cancer. It kills 50,000 Americans *every year*—nearly as many deaths as were produced during the whole nine-year period of the Vietnam War. Perhaps there is a reason for these dismal statistics: one-half kilogram (slightly more than one pound) of charcoal-broiled beef contains as much cancer-causing benzopyrene as 600 cigarettes!

And while we are on the subject, notice the cost savings in switching from meat to natural-protein sources. People have reported a food-bill savings of 40 percent by making this transition. In all probability, their medical bills will drop by an even larger amount over the coming years. They will be healthier, less dependent, and more able to live self-sufficiently because many of these foods are more easily stored (what deteriorates quicker than animal products?), helping to tide them over during food shortages or power failures.

A different diet! At first it may seem like a major adjustment to make. On reflection, all the arguments coming out of tomorrow seem to favor it. It's worth a try. Long ago the idea was disproved that meat was necessary for strength and endurance—that meat was essential for a balanced diet. Studies show that athletes on a non- or low-meat, high-carbohydrate diet actually have far more endurance than those who eat meat heavily. You can enjoy those advantages too.

As important as anything else we have said, adopt an attitude of quiet confidence. Some call it "positive thinking," or "possibility thinking." Be happy. Happiness is an amazingly powerful antidote to disease. The Good Book says, "A cheerful heart is a good medicine, but a downcast spirit dries up the bones." Proverbs 17:22, RSV.

In Breslow's study, unhappy people had a 55 to 60 percent higher death rate in the nine-year study than those who were generally happy. How does one attain the sometimes elusive goal of happiness—especially in a world that for so many seems to junk youthful dreams one way or another? You have already made a significant start by caring about the future and by doing something in an orderly, intelligent way toward preparing for it. But there is an even more powerful source of happiness. And that is a belief in a Supreme Being who knows the future and who cares about you. We will talk about Him in chapter 5.

Armed with such a faith, millions of people have faced history's worst challenges and survived. You can too—and the freedom from anxiety that you can enjoy is also a powerful aid in resisting the many emotion-related diseases that plague so many people in our unstable world. In fact, happy people have learned how to make stress work for them. Happy people are not the normal victims of stress-related troubles.

MAKING STRESS WORK FOR YOU

Stress can give you a diploma, a marvelous spouse, a happy family, and a handsome income. But stress also can give you headaches, hemorrhoids, and a heart attack. No one can avoid stress unless he or she chooses to die. The question then: How can we make stress work for and not against us?

Dr. Hans Selye, an endocrinologist who served for thirty-two years on the faculty of the University of Montreal, has been known as the world's foremost authority on stress since his first report in 1936. His best-known book, *Stress Without Distress,* has been translated into at least eleven languages. Dr. Selye defines stress as the state of the body after any kind of demand or stimulation. Such demands (causes of stress) as heat and cold are obvious and can be directly satisfied. But emotional stressors are more difficult to pinpoint and thus more difficult to care for.

Medical research informs us that 80 percent or more of our common physical problems—such as colitis, constipation, diarrhea, hemorrhoids, back pains, insomnia, fatigue, high blood pressure, and the common cold—are emotional reactions to the stresses of life. And when a truly serious physical problem develops, the emotional reaction to external stressors has much to do with the speed of recovery.

When our emotional bank is overdrawn (that is, overstimulated), we must transfer energy from our savings account. When this is done too often within a short span of time, all kinds of physical problems begin to develop. And emotional signals, too, begin to flash—such as anger, sloppy work, and anxiety.

Because none of us can avoid all stress-producing factors, we should figure out a personal method of response. Even happy events, such as graduations, vacations, or a new job, drain the nervous system, calling for higher spurts of adrenaline. Whatever the cause, when one is psychobiologically exhausted, stress occurs, or even depression!

For those experiencing anxiety or depression, many physicians are recommending a good B-complex vitamin—taken two or three times a day after meals—with increased intake of calcium and magnesium as well.

Daily exercise is specifically recommended, because recent research indicates that vigorous exercise stimulates the release of mood-elevating chemicals in the brain called endorphins. Endorphins function much as morphine does, without the negative side effects. Remember how much better you felt after returning from a half-hour jog or fast walk? This anxiety releaser was an added bonus to all the benefits exercise gave your heart and digestive system.

But we can do even more. We can recognize the difference between short-term stress and long-term stress. Most of us can handle short-term stress fairly well—especially if we already have a healthy body. The problem with long-term stress is that its cause or causes never seem to let up. Such stresses might include family problems, a job that you seem locked into, or insufficient funds in an inflationary age. Our bodies are not set up to handle long-term chronic stress. Our bodies need "time off." We may find many ways to say, "Stop the world; I want to get off." Obesity, alcoholic binges, credit-card splurges, heart attacks, and nervous breakdowns are all negative reactions to long-term stress.

Psychologists tell us that the survivors are those who stand back and look at their health-damaging patterns. They decide to step out of the stream that seems to drive them along, willy-nilly. They may not want or be able to change their environment or job or family—but they can change themselves and the way they permit life to control them. They begin to say, "I will pay attention to my health. I will not let somebody else ruin me. I will feel more satisfied taking a walk than eating so much. I will do one thing today that helps somebody else. I will not tackle all my jobs at once—I will take them one at a time. Just as a bank teller does, I too have a right to shut my window sometime during the day."

So we figure out how to change our life-style in order to handle our share of stress when it comes. We reduce the negative flow into our system where we can, such as the hours in front of the television or listening to the radio, or the time spent with certain people who only add to our physical and emotional drain. For many, simply discovering that they can choose what they may do with their leisure time—that they are not as controlled by their spouses or parents or children as they had once thought—is all a tremendous relief!

Furthermore, simply discovering that hidden guilt is at the bottom of most restlessness and anxiety and asking for forgiveness has proved to be marvelous therapy for thousands.

Estimates indicate that Americans alone will spend hundreds of millions of dollars on tranquilizers this year. More than $230 billion dollars is spent annually in America on health-care services. Probably most readers of these pages will spend some part of this awesome expense on themselves—perhaps needlessly.

But the survivor has decided to take charge wherever he has a choice. Those men or women who face the future with a survival mentality know that they will need every advantage working for them. Remember: *Tomorrow is not for the weak—only the fit survive.*

A Survival Attitude

You have now begun to build your survival plan on the most solid possible foundation—your own good health. You have learned the basics about how a better diet and life-style can increase your survival chances. But you have only begun.

The next step is to develop a survival attitude. Now it is time to think in terms of your own personal resourcefulness. To a larger degree than you may have thought, you can control your future. You need not be a helpless victim of what many call fate—at least as long as life lasts.

What would be your thoughts should you hear that someone has decided to run across an entire continent? And suppose that such a person has only one leg?

Pictured in national newspapers and magazines in the summer and fall of 1980, Terry Fox began his long-distance feat on April 12 in St. John's, Newfoundland, and headed for Vancouver, British Columbia—5300 miles away.

Three and a half years before, bone cancer had been discovered, requiring that his right leg be amputated above the knee. This blow seemed to rule out forever any further athletic achievements—such as he had already attained in soccer and basketball at Simon Fraser University near Vancouver.

But Terry Fox did not give up. He listened to medical counsel, concluding that in his war with cancer, the odds might be against him. Yet he still had life and desire. Whatever time he had left, he would use to help others.

The Canadian Cancer Society sponsored his run with a fund-raising program. Wearing a white T-shirt labeled "Marathon of Hope," Terry said, "I wanted to show people that just because they're disabled, it's not the end."—*Time*, September 15, 1980, p. 76.

So he ran. Crowds of cheering countrymen in towns and cities across eastern Canada turned out as he ran by. In Toronto, 10,000 honored his gutsy determination.

On good days Terry covered thirty miles. In the early days he ran through rain, snow, and hailstones. During the summer he endured the blistering afternoon heat. A welder was needed at one point to spot-weld repairs on his artificial leg.

For well-wishers, it was not easy to see Terry's bloody stump or watch his grim face as it reflected the pain he suffered.

Then in early September, Terry Fox conceded. The race was over—3336 miles from his starting point, more than halfway to his goal. Three miles outside Thunder Bay, Ontario, Terry was wracked with a cough and pain in his neck and chest. He bravely ran on, not wanting to disappoint the waiting spectators. But after checking into a local hospital for tests, he learned what he had feared—his cancer had spread.

Nevertheless, nearly $2 million in pledges for cancer research had been raised. His life probably shortened, Terry Fox had yet made his point. He had lifted the courage of millions, showed us all how to face tough times, and added to the day when cancer may be as forgotten as smallpox or diphtheria.

Promising to finish the race someday, Terry flew home to Vancouver, after these parting words: "I've lived one day at a time before, and I will now." During the next few months collections were taken in restaurants, bars, and other businesses across Canada. A Canada-wide telethon brought in more than $10 million. Although Terry lost his fight against cancer in June, 1981, he had raised $24 million for research to combat his killer. In final tribute, for two years in succession, Terry Fox was voted "Canadian of the Year," 1980, 1981.

Each of us may think of some reason why he or she can't succeed. But survivors don't look at what they don't have—only at what they do. And most of us have more than Terry Fox had. Let's begin by building on what we have.

For a start, go to Appendix B and look over the list of books we have recommended on diet and health. Pick out two or three and continue reading. Make it a family project—each person researching and sharing his newfound ideas with the family group. Set aside some time—perhaps an evening or a weekend afternoon—in which the family can share new ideas about how to improve the quality of family life. It could involve a new way to enjoy weekends. Whatever, you have embarked on a program in which you are limited only by your imagination and initiative. You'll be surprised to learn how much the family can benefit from the energy and enthusiasm of its younger members. When everyone participates with creative thought, you'll find greater cooperation—and possibly greater family unity—than you've ever enjoyed before.

You may have already discovered that thinking prudently about tomorrow has a spillover effect which benefits the present as much as it will your future. That may be best illustrated with our next survival rule. In Step One you learned that "only the fit survive." Step Two builds on Step One—in most crises, *only the useful survive*.

Particularly in times of natural catastrophe or financial hardship (a depression, a deep recession, or personal reverses), those who best survive are those who are most indispensable to their fellow beings.

Let's illustrate. Whom would you rather live next door to: someone who is charming, witty, and friendly; or someone who is charming, witty, friendly, and has taken the Red Cross first-aid course? When the chips are down, during the panic of a crisis, *usefulness* matters most.

Take a few moments and inventory your life. How truly useful and resourceful are you at home, in your neighborhood, on the job? If you were to leave, would you be quickly forgotten, your place easily taken by others? Or would you leave a void so hard to fill that people would long for your return? After a little thought, you can figure your own usefulness quotient. Fortunately, you have the time and opportunity to improve your odds. Usefulness is a survival tool you can build into your life immediately.

In fact, you have already begun. In tomorrow's challenges (and there will be many) most people will not have the health advantages you have already begun to put into practice. Even in your present job, most of your co-workers will not have the competitive edge that a sound health program gives you.

But there is much more, and before this chapter is over you'll probably agree that survival planning may be the best thing that ever happened to your present career.

Some years ago a successful financier gave some advice on how to make a million dollars. His suggestion was framed in six simple words: "Find a need and fill it." An easy rule—a profound effect. The greater the need you are able to fill, the greater your reward—and the greater your probability of surviving, whether in your field of employment or family finance or in the larger sphere of human relations.

Begin Step Two with a new outlook on the world you touch every day. Where are the real needs, and how can you personally fill them? Discipline your mind to watch for opportunities to be useful. Forget about the clock and about merely satisfying the minimal expectations of others. See your world not as it is, but as it may be—with a little extra help from you. To those who tend to be intimidated or conditioned by big government, big business, big labor, or mass entertainment, that may seem like a strange outlook at first. After all, some say, what can one person do? But give it a try. We think you'll find it brings new zest to life and will dramatically change the way people regard you.

You ask, How can I really make a difference? By realizing that your first obligation, to yourself, to your community, and to your God, is self-development. No, we are not advocating a self-centered, you-are-number-one attitude. On the contrary, we are simply saying that one of the most potent aspects of survival insurance is the usefulness you build into your life-style. From the larger viewpoint, those who are growing daily in capability and usefulness are fulfilling their purpose for existence. All the while, their survival probabilities are quietly improving.

So begin now to "save" for tomorrow—and we are now talking about something far broader than accumulating a bank account. Instead, concentrate on investing in yourself. Watch for every opportunity to *learn something new and useful*. Take the next few weekends and master basic electrical and plumbing skills. Figure out how to grow fruit and vegetables in a small area and how to improve the soil. Look for unmet needs, and devise ways to solve them. Concentrate on making yourself as indispensable as possible, not for shallow, egocentric reasons, but for the joy of filling the needs of others with ever-increasing competence. Someone in your family, your neighborhood, your church, at your job is the one person to whom others instinctively turn when they need help with important problems. If you are that person, then your survival quotient is already high. If not, shouldn't you think about becoming that person? For their sakes?

Remember that there is a difference between good intentions and *competence*. Let's illustrate. At the scene of an accident, many people would like to help; few know how. Wringing one's hands in sympathy is not the same as using those hands to stop bleeding. Yet all standing by could have been useful, if they had devoted a few hours to a first-aid class. Think it through, and you'll realize that the same principle applies on a very broad scale to all phases of your life. Tomorrow holds a spectrum of risks so great that you cannot guess from which direction the challenge will come.

What if a member of your family should be seriously hurt and no immediate medical help were available except for what you are able to give? With your present state of preparedness, would you be able to do much more than wring your hands and wish for their recovery?

What if you should have to rebuild your home or create new shelter with little or no assistance? Before you dismiss these questions as implausible fiction, recognize that you could face them in the real world with almost no warning. Neighborhood fire, earthquakes, hurricanes, and economic depressions have a sudden way of altering the most comfortable living conditions. You could even face an unknown challenge with stunning suddenness in the middle of your next airline trip. Preparedness pays.

You may be a parent with a child facing adolescence. How much time have you devoted to learning about adolescent stress? Would you recognize a problem? Most parents wouldn't. A parent who prepares by reading and attending classes to understand energetic teenagers is already reducing future hazards and grief. For such parents, self-development is surely their first duty to their children.

So you should ask yourself these questions: How useful am I? How many kinds of problems can I personally solve? If those questions find your inventory a little lower than you'd like, then be glad you're thinking about it now rather than finding out the hard way.

Remember that you can't give more than you have. Only those who have done their homework can solve the problem, pass the test, or be recommended by others who have learned to trust their work. Self-development is surely our first duty to God and man. Usefulness in service is the acid test of whether the self-development is loving or selfish.

Preparing yourself for tomorrow will, of course, cost you something today. Something such as not spending your whole paycheck and putting some of it aside in a savings account. Increasing your usefulness may cut into your tennis time or get you off the couch and away from the television. Spend some evenings at a community college learning about gardening or construction or basic first aid. Keep exercising till you can run or swim a mile. Or walk a fifteen-minute mile. Then start on the second mile. Take a course in nature study so that on your next outing you can make your children's (or grandchildren's) world come alive.

Give some of your time to others. Organize parent-study groups at your church. Look around your neighborhood for the sick or aged who may need some special yard work or house repair. Put your newfound skills to practical use. Think of how many people will be cheered. Do you see what is happening? You are bettering the world around you while your own future becomes more secure, because you are better prepared for its inevitable surprises.

If, like most people, you have grown accustomed to enjoying the present while largely ignoring tomorrow's potential problems, these suggestions may at first seem a bit irksome. You may feel like an overweight person starting a new diet—you want results, but you don't particularly enjoy what you have to go through to get them.

In reality you are starting a diet—a time and energy diet, in which you are trading in an old and flabby life-style for something very new. You will be imposing upon yourself disciplines which you probably haven't endured for years, and it is only natural for that part of you which likes comfort to rebel. Don't be surprised, therefore, if fairly early in the program you encounter what may seem like an overwhelming urge to quit, to forget all this effort and let tomorrow worry about itself. Runners call it "hitting the wall." When that urge to stop comes, give your spirit that extra kick, and you will discover something wonderful about yourself. This is the one test that separates the survivors from the unprepared. As Goethe put it, "Everybody wants to be somebody; nobody wants to grow." Exaggerated, perhaps, but you can be among the exceptions who even now are ensuring both short- and long-term survival.

Can the world forget those who survived the horror of Nazi concentration camps or Russian labor camps? Untold millions survived in spirit until they were overtaken by death. Think of those who would share scraps of bread, always dividing with their fellow inmates. Think of the length to which men and women would go to keep their minds occupied. We tremble at the price so many paid to provide even the slightest comforts for others.

Aleksandr Solzhenitsyn has put us all in his debt with his heart-wrenching recital of life in the desolate Siberian wastelands, where so many tens of thousands still live today—often with less than animal privileges. He tells about suddenly discovering the joy of writing after six gloomy years when he hit "the hard, rocky bottom." Then it happened: "Sometimes in a sullen work party with Tommy-gunners barking about me, lines and images crowded in so urgently that I felt myself borne through the air, overleaping the column in my hurry to reach the work site and find a corner to write. At such moments I was both free and happy."

But how could he write when prisoners were searched constantly? He learned something about memory: "No longer burdened with frivolous and superfluous knowledge, a prisoner's memory is astonishingly capacious, and can expand indefinitely."

He would "write snatches of twelve to twenty lines

at a time, polish them, learn them by heart, and burn them. . . . Every fiftieth and every hundredth line I memorized with special care, to help me keep count. Once a month I recited all that I had written. If the wrong line came out in place of one of the hundreds or fifties, I went over it all again and again until I caught the slippery fugitives.'' By the end of his prison sentence, Solzhenitsyn had accumulated 12,000 memorized lines, which he quickly reproduced on paper when he was finally released. (See *The Gulag Archipelago,* vol. 3, pp. 98-111.)

So the world today knows, perhaps for the first time, how brutal, how ruthless, the state can become in trying to crush the spirit of millions of its own people—and not merely the enemy with foreign tongue. But the telling impact of Solzhenitsyn in his several volumes is not merely in his dreary recital of horror. You will find the distant chorus of brave men and women whose spiritual strength rose higher than their torment as in too many cases they resisted unto death.

Some of the most creative men and women alive today—in music, art, religion, law, business, and medicine—are survivors. Far from being reduced to purely materialistic robots as the ''system'' had planned, these survivors are living exhibits that the experiment failed. Solzhenitsyn himself was exiled from his homeland because he cried out so loudly. Along with many others, he proved that we were made to survive incredible circumstances if we utilize personal resources, and especially if we permit divine resources to flow into our lives.

In Step Two we have been discussing a survival attitude. We have been talking about developing personal resources—not just the material, but also those aspects we call spiritual, such as love, caring, integrity, and responsibility. We have noted that we can't possess such qualities unless they are expressed in ways meaningful to others.

And you are doing all this in a way that does not and need not depend on a materialistic crutch. The American hostages in Tehran had plenty of weapons at their disposal and plenty of food—no doubt some of it freeze-dried! They had all the materialistic props you could hope for in a survival plan. But when the challenge came, all this seemed to vanish, leaving them with nothing but their personal competence and inner strength. So it was in Vietnam's Hanoi Hilton and among the Korean conflict prisoners of war. So it will be in the major crises in your future.

Both the Iranian hostages and the POWs learned during their ordeals that when the pressure is on— when we seem to be truly alone with no relief in sight— we quickly realize our need of an ally called *faith*. When times are easy, we tend to be very independent and self-sufficient. Under pressure, most survivors relearn the meaning of faith—the belief that a Divine Being cares about us. Few things are so lonely as facing a great personal crisis without the hope that comes from faith in a God who cares. We'll talk about this in succeeding chapters.

So Step Two is to develop the attitude of a survivor—to prepare each day so that you are better equipped than yesterday to store within yourself a growing array of ways to find and meet human needs. Good health, an active and solution-oriented mind, a growing list of ways in which you may serve others better, an inner strength that can face challenges without leaning on material crutches or even on other people, a deepening trust in God that welds all these qualities together—what better combination of traits could you possibly offer your own future? Or your children?

The Bible describes those who truly survive. In this passage you will recognize that such people have understood Step Two of our survival plan.

"When the Son of man comes in his glory, and all the angels with him, then he will sit on his glorious throne. Before him will be gathered all the nations, and he will separate them one from another as a shepherd separates the sheep from the goats, and he will place the sheep at his right hand, but the goats at the left. Then the King will say to those at his right hand, 'Come, O blessed of my Father, inherit the kingdom prepared for you from the foundation of the world; for I was hungry and you gave me food, I was thirsty and you gave me drink, I was a stranger and you welcomed me, I was naked and you clothed me, I was sick and you visited me, I was in prison and you came to me.'

"Then the righteous will answer him, 'Lord, when did we see thee hungry and feed thee, or thirsty and give thee drink? And when did we see thee a stranger and welcome thee, or naked and clothe thee? And when did we see thee sick or in prison and visit thee?'

"And the King will answer them, 'Truly, I say to you, as you did it to one of the least of these my brethren, you did it to me.' " Matthew 25:31-40, RSV.

Remember: *Tomorrow is not for the weak—only the fit, the useful, the loving survive.*

A Survival Life-style

Time now to talk about survival planning in a material way: home, personal safety, and economic strategy. We may as well admit it. Economically, as well as in many other ways, we are headed for deep trouble. If you are retired, your fixed income buys less and less, because inflation forces prices higher and higher. If you are still working, you are probably contributing to a retirement plan that sounds good in today's dollars but may not even be viable when you need it. The most knowledgeable economic forecasters see no plausible solution to high-deficit government spending and the inevitable inflationary fallout. This double battering from inflationary prices and higher taxes (often hidden) erodes earning power today and makes saving for the future seem as old-fashioned as the 35¢ gallon of gas or the 10¢ subway ride.

Even the wealthy skitter nervously from gold to diamonds to works of art, trying to put their money into something that will hold some value. We have reached a point where politically, militarily, and economically, anything can happen—a time without historical parallels—and the best-informed people already know that.

What hope is there for the average individual to steer safely through the economic minefields? Or the fallout of social unrest? Plenty—*if* you are prepared to adopt some life-style changes which minimize your risk.

First, let's talk about the major risks you face. If you are a typical city dweller, you face a number of growing threats:

Exposure to a high incidence of crime.

Disruption of vital commodities and services during a strike or natural crisis.

Unnecessarily high dependence on a deteriorating economy.

Air and water pollution. (For example, many medical experts fear that the seeds for disabling lung disease have already been sown for millions.)

Undesirable danger during times of disorder.

More dangers exist, of course, but we think these are the most obvious. Each confronts you with an unacceptably high risk of loss or personal harm. At times they may seem to join hands and surround you. Yet our research indicates that they can be minimized much more easily than you might think—and with rules that are as sensible and easy to follow as those we gave you in Step One (Chapter 2) when we discussed positive steps to reduce the risk of disease.

Remember that we are approaching survival from the standpoint of nature's rules, and nature tends toward simple, direct, and very sensible solutions: The future belongs to the prepared. Tomorrow is not for the weak. Only the fit and the useful survive.

How, then, can you minimize these various risks for you and your family? How and where should you live? How should you prepare economically? As we researched these very practical questions about personal preparedness, we concluded that the best and most modern advice comes from one of the oldest books known to mankind—a book in which human survival is one of its major themes.

This book tells about man's successes and failures from the dawn of history, weaving in commonsense lessons learned in times of great stress and personal danger. It also has passages describing our present world so vividly that to read them gives one an almost eerie sense of déjà vu.

Here are some examples. See if you do not agree.

On society: "You must face the fact: the final age of this world is to be a time of troubles. Men will love nothing but money and self; they will be arrogant, boastful, and abusive; with no respect for parents, no gratitude, no piety, no natural affection; they will be implacable in their hatreds, scandal-mongers, intemperate and fierce, strangers to all goodness, traitors, adventurers, swollen with self-importance."

On the economy: "A word to you who have great possessions. Weep and wail over the miserable fate descending upon you. Your riches have rotted; your fine clothes are moth-eaten; your silver and gold have rusted away, and their very rust will be evidence against you and consume your flesh like fire. You have piled up wealth in an age that is near its close."

On world politics: "Nations will stand helpless . . . ; men will faint with terror at the thought of all that is coming upon the world."

An uncanny rightness pervades this book. Its stories out of history are as relevant as today's news. Its predictions about our day are vividly fulfilled. We have chosen to base this important chapter on the advice this books gives. It is called the Bible, and we quote it without apology. It is the clearest, most useful collection of advice on survival we were able to find.

Let's begin with a biblical survival story taken from the morning of human history—a story of two men, two attitudes, and two life-styles, which ends in survival for one and tragedy for the other. The first man adopted the life-style we are ultimately going to recommend to you. He became immensely wealthy; and in a turbulent age, when safety could not be taken for granted, he lived remarkably undisturbed. So large were his reserves that when his friends faced invasion and slavery, he was able to intervene and secure their safety.

The other man chose a life-style which many people today also choose—an apparently easy life in an urban setting, surrounded with all the supposed advantages of convenience bordering on luxury—unaware that these attractions also contained the seeds of their own destruction. His choice cost him his wealth, his wife, and even the integrity of his daughter.

The story begins a little over 1900 years before Christ, somewhere southeast of present-day Jerusalem. The two men in our story, an uncle and his nephew, lived side by side. The older man was Abraham; the younger, Lot. Over the years they had become so wealthy that the land surrounding them could not adequately provide for the livestock of both men. As you might suspect, trouble broke out between their hired herdsmen.

One day the older man proposed a solution. "The whole country is there in front of you; let us part company. If you go left, I will go right; if you go right, I will go left." Genesis 13:9, NEB.

Though entitled by custom and courtesy to have first choice, Abraham yielded that privilege to his younger nephew. The choices Lot faced are basically the same that confront you. Before him stretched the plain of Sodom—well watered, green, fabulously wealthy, studded with three or four cities that seemed to offer all the comfort and ease a man or woman could desire. The other alternative lay to the northwest, in the quiet, folded hills of Judea. Here comparatively few people lived. Instead of urban excitement one could expect the challenges of the independent life.

Lot made his decision. He chose Sodom, with all its attractions and seeming security. True to his word, Abraham accepted the other alternative, and the men parted company. Little did either dream how dramatic their reunion would be.

Lot had chosen a superficially attractive alternative that contained some extremely high risks, had he cared to think about them. Temptingly wealthy, ill defended on a flat, grassy plain, Sodom was an extremely enticing target for greedy neighbors. Roving chieftains with professional soldiers roamed the plains of the Fertile Crescent looking for quick wealth and handy slaves. Given that set of circumstances, it was only a matter of time until Sodom would attract most unwelcome attention.

When the storm came, it was overwhelming. Whole groups of marauding kings combined their forces and swept through Sodom. Nearly everyone was carried off into slavery, including hapless Lot, who had chosen the easy life, only to discover that ease could be fragile in an unpredictable world.

Interestingly, the few people who escaped from the plunderers headed in the same direction Abraham had gone—toward the comforting seclusion of the hills rising west of their ransacked city. One of the stragglers, managing to reach Abraham's encampment, told an incoherent story of fighting and defeat, of breached walls and captives led off into a terror-filled night. What happened next speaks volumes about survival preparedness and the sort of life-style that rises to meet emergencies.

First of all, Abraham and his men were in excellent health. They had learned the first rule of survival—only the fit survive. In making personal health a very important aspect of their life-style they were well prepared for emergencies. Although they numbered only 318, they soon proved more than a match for a whole confederation of armies—and this after a forced march to catch up with the invaders.

Next, Abraham was prepared with the knowledge required to face an emergency; he did not have to stop during a crisis to learn survival skills, for they were already a part of his life-style. The brief biblical account pictures Abraham and his small force moving with amazing speed as they overtook the enemy. They attacked with such surprise and skill that they quickly defeated a much superior military force.

Then Abraham exhibited still another survival trait which helped to ensure his safety for years to come. After successfully returning the inhabitants of Sodom to their city, he refused their offer to take all the recovered wealth as a reward. He had no intention of profiting by a city's misfortune. Withdrawing again to his mountain home, he left behind an example of a generous spirit and a well-ordered life that knew how to survive.

That, incredibly, is not the end of the story. By this time warning flags were visible everywhere. Of all the people in comfortable Sodom, Lot should have been the first to alert his neighbors that their life-style could be most hazardous. Yet he and his neighbors chose to remain in Sodom, apparently anesthetized to the subtle way in which moral and social decay had numbed their judgment and moral perception.

That fact was ultimately brought most rudely to Lot's attention when he offered two wayfarers a night's lodging in his home. Attracted by the sight of these travelers, the Sodomites gathered outside Lot's door—and perhaps the story is best told by reading the biblical account:

"Before they lay down to sleep, the men of Sodom, both young and old, surrounded the house—everyone without exception. They called to Lot and asked him where the men were who had entered his house that night. 'Bring them out', they shouted, 'so that we can have intercourse with them.' " Genesis 19:4, 5, NEB.

The story of that night, Sodom's last on earth—of the supernatural blindness that fell upon these perverted men of Sodom, of the desperate flight of Lot and his family, and of the flaming destruction of the city—is all a part of biblical history. Warned by an angel, Lot fled the city with his wife and two unmarried daughters, escaping across the plain toward a smaller town where they hoped to find refuge. But Lot's wife still longed for the comforts and wealth she had left behind. In a fateful moment of indecision, contrary to the warning of the angel, she turned to watch as Sodom exploded. That delay cost her life.

Lot and his daughters, too terrified to look back, hastened on, briefly seeking shelter in the nearby city of Zoar, and then hurrying on to the shelter of the mountains, where they finally hid in a cave—penniless, bereaved, the perfect picture of twentieth-century refugees.

Now the tragedy compounded itself. Having exposed his daughters to an environment where morality was low—where situation ethics and human desires determined moral decision making—Lot should have expected what would happen next, except that it was a perversion too gross for a father to envision. The daughters, apparently concerned that Lot's male descendents were dead in Sodom, decided to preserve his posterity. After making him drunk, they each became pregnant by him.

And so we find Lot, the one-time millionaire, now a ragged refugee in a cave, his wife dead, his possessions gone, his daughters carrying his children—as complete a scene of wretchedness as anyone could dream up to horrify the mind. And all because of a decision that put short-term ease ahead of long-term benefits.

The biblical account is starkly realistic. It softens nothing, even for the sake of gentility. And it is amazingly up-to-date. Lot's experience depicts what millions—hundreds of millions—will yet face in the near future: foreign invasion, loss of all possessions, death of loved ones, homelessness, even children stained by immorality.

Yet none of these catastrophes were forced upon Lot. *His calamities were merely the ultimate consequences of his choice of life-style*.

Let's return now to Abraham and compare how his life-style affected his ability to react to emergencies and his ability to survive. First, Abraham did not expose himself to unnecessary risk. True, life at first may have seemed easier on the fertile plain, where pastures were plentiful, goods and services were readily available, and the rigor of independent living did not have to be faced. Yet the absence of those apparent advantages of familiar Sodom, coupled with the challenge of the hill country, made Abraham strong.

Though a demanding life, it was filled with the things that mattered most: good health, self-reliance, freedom from artificial worries, and the opportunity to see in nature and his own personal experience the evidences of a Divine Being who could help him through any challenge or surprise. Year after year he saw nature itself respond successfully to challenge—always resilient, never giving up. He discovered that God fulfilled His promises, that peace, courage, and love followed whenever he submitted himself to his Lord's will. All this gave him the mightiest of all survival tools—something called faith.

Let's summarize the advantages of Abraham's rural, less-dependent lifestyle.

Avoidance of unnecessary risks, such as crime. In Sodom, Abraham would have subjected himself and his family to the risks of theft, military invasion, even slavery. He would ultimately have been trapped by the very luxuries that tempted him. By trading off these illusory benefits for a more natural life-style, he avoided dangers which brought ruin to his nephew.

Enough self-sufficiency to survive when essential goods and services are destroyed. We do not know the extent to which Abraham may have depended on outside goods and services, but we do know he was relatively self-sufficient. At the same time, Abraham was not a hermit. The biblical account indicates that he was well known and, no doubt, highly respected. The refugees from Sodom felt confident enough to seek him out.

Abraham chose to live near enough to society to be of service when needed, yet far enough away to minimize risk—whether it be moral, economic, or even civil. Thus he had a reserve out of which he could sustain his own household as well as his distressed neighbors when trouble came. He may not have had easy access to the marketplace, yet that fact gave him an independence that could survive when the marketplace was destroyed.

Avoidance of unnecessarily bad influences for the family–particularly for children. Notice the dramatic difference between Lot's children and Abraham's son. With the exception of two unmarried daughters, all of Lot's children were killed in the destruction of Sodom. His two daughters had become so insidiously corrupted by the immorality of their environment that they could ultimately commit incest while claiming they had "good motives." Biblical history tells us that the children they bore by their father became the progenitors of fierce and warlike tribes that ultimately pillaged Palestine and caused centuries of difficulties for the Jewish nation.

Abraham's son, Isaac—reared in the atmosphere of more natural surroundings—was a model of loyalty, obedience, and courage. Through him sprang the great Jewish nation. It is probably impossible to overstate the importance of neighborhood influences on children.

Personal safety during times of disorder. When Sodom was ransacked, Abraham's home and possessions appear to have remained free from danger. He owned considerable wealth that might have seemed easy plunder. Why was he by-passed?

First, he had great faith in divine protection. But he augmented that faith in a very practical way—his life-style was not the sort that attracted greedy notice. Wealthy though he was, he lived quietly in the country, ready to help when needed but not conspicuous with his possessions. And thus he minimized danger to himself and his family. No doubt he also had a reputation for alertness and common sense that gave roaming marauders second thoughts.

Economic independence. We do not know a great deal about the regional economy in Abraham's time, except to say that when the city of Sodom was destroyed, its wealth went with it. Had Abraham been dependent upon the economy of Sodom, he might have been financially wiped out in one night. Perhaps the best evidence of his financial independence was his refusal of Sodom's wealth when it was offered to him as a reward. We can infer that while he was responsive to the needs of his nearby urban neighbors, he did not unwisely depend on their shaky financial structure for his future security.

Perhaps it has occurred to you that all of Abraham's survival advantages correspond with the list at the start of this chapter which described the risks we face today. Except for one that seems to be a uniquely twentieth-century problem—air and water pollution. Yet even this risk can be minimized in the same way one minimizes the others.

And it has also probably occurred to you that the one basic technique for avoiding all these hazards is to adopt a simpler life-style, separated to a degree from the artificial problems posed by urbanization.

Does that mean that the solution to your problems is to "escape"? Many survival writers think so, some going so far as to advocate isolated living in your own moated world, protected by miles of wilderness. It all sounds attractive, but it is also very fictitious. Reality reminds us that there is no place to hide anymore—technology and military hardware have seen to that. So has commerce. If you could find an isolated place in which to hide, chances are some morning you'd be awakened by the thunder of logging trucks or oil-exploration crews working just across the valley. Stay put long enough, and you'd see housing subdivision signs. No, survival no longer means escape from risk. Rather, it means learning to minimize risk—and to meet it with personal and spiritual strength when it cannot be avoided.

Like Abraham of 4000 years ago, you, too, can avoid unnecessary risks. Let's go back to the Bible's survival suggestions and see how.

First, we'll talk about economics. "You must face the fact," the Bible warns, "the final age of this world is to be a time of troubles." 2 Timothy 3:1, NEB. It also foretells a time when wealth will disappear in a series of catastrophes. "A word to you who have great possessions. Weep and wail over the miserable fate descending upon you. Your riches have rotted; . . . your silver and gold have rusted away." James 5:1, 2, NEB. We'll shortly discuss these predictions in greater detail.

The Bible has no assurance for those who face the future with faith only in material resources. Instead, a storm unrelenting in its fury is forecast.

The wisest man who ever lived warns us that a "prudent man sees danger and hides himself; but the simple go on, and suffer for it." Proverbs 22:3. RSV. We need not fool ourselves, as most economists now admit, that our deteriorating economy is headed for any permanent, long-term recovery. Because of this reality facing all of us, the Bible has a number of suggestions on prudent economic planning. And they are all premised on the most vital of all natural laws: the only way to survive is to give.

" 'There was a rich man whose land yielded heavy crops,' " Christ said in one of His famous parables. " 'He debated with himself: "What am I to do? I have not the space to store my produce. This is what I will do," said he: "I will pull down my storehouses and build them bigger. I will collect in them all my corn and other goods, and then say to myself, 'Man, you have plenty of good things laid by, enough for many years: take life easy, eat, drink, and enjoy yourself.' " But

God said to him: "You fool, this very night you must surrender your life; you have made your money—who will get it now?" That is how it is with the man who amasses wealth for himself and remains a pauper in the sight of God.' " Luke 12:17-21, NEB.

What are we to make of that story? We think Jesus was emphasizing a fundamental fact of life itself. From the cell upward, life depends on the cycle of giving and receiving, of taking life's benefits only that they can be enhanced and passed on. Whenever that cycle is interrupted, death is the ultimate result.

When a lake cannot get rid of its inflow, toxic salts begin to concentrate until it cannot sustain life—as in Palestine's famed Dead Sea.

When a human cell ceases to work cooperatively with the rest of the human system, yet is vigorous in its own growth, it becomes a rapidly multiplying outlaw called cancer—and it ultimately destroys itself by killing the organism in which it lives.

"A generous man grows fat and prosperous," said Solomon, "and he who refreshes others will himself be refreshed. He who withholds his grain is cursed by the people. . . . Whoever relies on his wealth is riding for a fall." Proverbs 11:25-28, NEB.

So the first rule of economic survival is one which, to our materialistically conditioned ears, may sound illogical: *generosity*. Think about that principle for a few moments, however, and it becomes logical indeed. In times of major social crisis, for example, those who fare the worst are usually those who are perceived as being the "big spenders"—the most conspicuously affluent.

In fact, many who closely guard their wealth are actually nonfunctional consumers. So it was with a well-known French king during the French Revolution whose decorative but out-of-touch wife seemed unable to comprehend that the people of Paris were starving. Both of them went to the guillotine.

The most conspicuous consumers have fared badly in the major revolutions of eastern Europe, Asia, and Central and South America during this century. It is the functional, giving person who is more likely to survive. And that can involve not only his personal safety but his economic welfare as well. Once again, Solomon said it best: "A man may spend freely and yet grow richer; another is sparing beyond measure, yet ends in poverty." Proverbs 11:24, NEB.

At this point you may be asking yourself again whether you're really reading a book about survival. Are all those writers wrong who urge you to stockpile large quantities of food and merchandise and to learn how to use a gun? Is it possible that the Bible's apparently illogical suggestions can pull you through, when guns, freeze-dried food, and concrete cannot?

Before you answer that question too quickly, remember France's massive Maginot Line, outflanked by panzers in a matter of days. What ultimately saved France and the free world was not that obsolete line of concrete and steel. It was, rather, the spirit of the French people and their Allies who awakened to the challenge and were willing to give more than they had dreamed of giving when times were easy.

Perhaps it is all said best in the words of Jesus, whose advice wipes away a thousand worries. "Think of the lilies: they neither spin nor weave; yet I tell you, even Solomon in all his splendour was not attired like one of these. But if that is how God clothes the grass, which is growing in the field today, and tomorrow is thrown on the stove, how much more will he clothe you! . . . And so you are not to set your mind on

food and drink; you are not to worry. For all these
are things for the heathen to run after; but you have a
Father who knows that you need them. No, set your
mind upon his kingdom, and all the rest will come to
you as well." Luke 12:27-31, NEB.

"My God shall supply all your need," another Bible
writer noted (Philippians 4:19); and the prophet Isaiah,
700 years before Christ, described the real survival fortress which people should be preparing: "The man
who lives an upright life and speaks the truth, who
scorns to enrich himself by extortion, who snaps his
fingers at a bribe, who stops his ears to hear nothing of
bloodshed, who closes his eyes to the sight of evil—
that is the man who shall dwell on the heights, his refuge a fastness in the cliffs, his bread secure and his
water never failing." Isaiah 33:15, 16, NEB. In our
opinion, every wilderness retreat, every cache of
hoarded possessions, is merely a counterfeit of the real
fortress Isaiah described so graphically twenty-seven
centuries ago.

In the meantime, the Bible has some practical suggestions on managing your money. If persons in need
of funds wish to borrow from you and you are able to
accommodate them, by all means do so. But for your
own part, avoid debt. "You will lend to . . . many nations," God told his people long ago, "but you yourselves will not borrow." Deuteronomy 15:6, NEB. Obviously, borrowing may be necessary at times,
especially to finance such large items as a home or
automobile, which, in themselves, provide collateral.
But one's future security is always better when borrowing is minimized. Avoid putting too much of your
money into investments which leave you dependent on
(and sometimes entangled in) an economy that is in serious trouble. Wise Solomon also wrote, "The bor-

rower becomes the lender's slave." Proverbs 22:7, NEB.

The life of Abraham illustrates what we are talking about. No evidence exists that he lost money because of imprudent investments in Sodom. Whatever else he may have owned, it is clear that he had the tools and materials needed to maintain reasonable self-sufficiency for his family during critical times.

We think the biblical lessons emphasize a life pattern of frugality and diligence. This implies investing one's surplus funds in personal skills as well as in the tools and supplies one needs for reasonable self-reliance. It certainly includes prudent investment in a rural area where you and your family can enjoy a better life-style while minimizing risks. We think it does not include garages filled with hoards of materials you may never need and which only serve to attract the very dangers you fear most. "Do not be anxious about tomorrow," Christ advised; "tomorrow will look after itself. Each day has troubles enough of its own." Matthew 6:34, NEB. We think that is sage advice indeed in the uncertain and ever-changing world of economics.

Next, let's talk about your choice of life-style: where and how to live. It is evident from biblical and secular history that the areas of highest risk are those which are most urban. Somehow, when men and women or animals overconcentrate, living too closely together, trouble quickly follows. Often this fact has been demonstrated and studied in research projects. Diseases, physical and emotional, rapidly increase, depending on the compactness of living conditions.

We have already seen that all six of today's major risks can be minimized by choosing a simpler life-style which emphasizes rural freedom and a degree of independence from the overstressed economic system.

For many people, of course, this may be a difficult dream to realize.

One of the worst moves you can make is to plunge mindlessly into a rural setting without adequate thought about income sources for you and your family. For this reason we stress prudence: move carefully; plan before you leap. "Would any of you think of building a tower without first sitting down and calculating the cost, to see whether he could afford to finish it?" Jesus asked. "Otherwise, if he has laid its foundation and then is not able to complete it, all the onlookers will laugh at him. 'There is the man', they will say, 'who started to build and could not finish.' " Luke 14:28-31, NEB.

Yet the advantages of rural life are overwhelming. In contact with nature, free from much of the pollution of city life, free also from the moral pollution that pervades so many cities, one enjoys the greatest degree of liberty possible on earth. While it may not be practical to seek total self-sufficiency in a rural setting, one can survive minicrises such as strikes or shortages with far less stress. In such a setting, children grow up watching the natural world cooperate with man's work and care—a living lesson in the natural rule of taking only to give again. In the very morning of human history, God placed the newly created human couple in a beautiful garden. It is difficult to improve on the original plan.

Remember that we earlier referred to the Loma Linda University study of that large control group with their remarkably low disease rates. We have already discussed how their diet appears to be a factor in reducing disease risks. But two other diseases, which we commonly associate with life-style, also show that this group has a significant advantage. Their death rate from peptic ulcers is only 42 percent of the average. Another study showed their average blood pressure levels to be significantly lower than the average. Since those conditions are often associated with life-style, let's take a look at some of their thinking.

For years this group has listened to such counsel as this: "Instead of the crowded city, seek some retired situation where your children will be, so far as possible, shielded from temptation, and there train and educate them for usefulness. . . . Life in the cities is false and artificial. The intense passion for money getting, the whirl of excitement and pleasure seeking, the thirst for display, the luxury and extravagance, all are forces that, with the great masses of mankind, are turning the mind from life's true purpose. . . . The more nearly we come into harmony with God's original plan, the more favorable will be our position to secure health of body, and mind, and soul."

But their emphasis has not been on retreat. This world-wide group, representing all levels of society, is not composed of escapists—especially when we note that they maintain one of the largest chains of health-care institutions in the world. Most of them simply believe that, whenever possible, country living offers too many benefits to turn down.

Here is more of their philosophy: "An active, out-of-door life would develop health of both mind and body. They would have a garden to cultivate, where they might find both amusement and useful employment. The training of plants and flowers tend to the improvement of taste and judgment, while an acquaintance with God's useful and beautiful creations has a refining and ennobling influence upon the mind, referring it to the Maker and Master of all."

"A return to simpler methods will be appreciated by

the children and youth. Work in the garden and field
will be an agreeable change from the wearisome routine of abstract lessons, to which their young minds
should never be confined. To the nervous child, who
finds lessons from books exhausting and hard to remember, it will be especially valuable. There is
health and happiness for him in the study of nature;
and the impressions made will not fade out of his mind,
for they will be associated with objects that are contin-
ually before his eyes.''

Unfortunately, not everyone can immediately
change the location of his home—no matter how ear-
nest he or she may be. A combination of work opportunity and financial limitations may postpone the family's move to a more wholesome rural environment.
Are we saying anything to such families? Yes, indeed.

No matter where one lives, the premium will be on
the survivor in the months and years ahead. But those
who live in our cities realize that such principles are
even more needed by them than others.

We see these principles at work in such programs as
the Neighborhood Watch and the volunteer food and
travel assistance services some communities are noted
for. Should neighbors not know who may be incapaci-
tated by illness or accident in their area? Where else
but in the city could the survivor principle or usefulness be more needed? In fact, certain crowded neighborhoods have developed a remarkable spirit of unity
and self-protection, when their members have realized
that they alone can solve their potential problems.

We are not suggesting that urban survivalists should
live as if in a besieged fortress. Not at all. While
survivalists are keenly aware of obvious threats to
their physical and moral well-being, they have their
eyes wide open to the pleasant features still available in

the city. Although parents may wish for a "home in the country," they can still open to their children the wonders found in most city parks and zoos. The lift and exhilaration of a Mozart concert or the free excitement of frequent visits to the library are valuable compensations to an alert urban survivalist.

We are simply saying that survivalists will think positively, constructively, and prudently about whatever circumstances they find themselves in; they will move from the good to the better to the best—as circumstances arise.

Survivalists are realists who listen carefully to the fundamentals learned from past experiences. They realize that the challenges of the 1980s are many and complex, defying the proposed solutions of the world's best-trained minds. Economists now admit that they cannot solve the modern complexities that wobble between depression and inflation. Nor can tacticians or police guarantee your safety. Politicians cannot legislate stability. But *you* can solve all these problems to a remarkable degree simply by adopting, when possible, a simpler life-style away from urban risks and by living the sort of useful life that makes you valuable both in the eyes of man and God. With this, and with a faith in God's protection, you have a wall of safety that will survive when concrete and modern technology fail.

And now you are ready for the final step in planning your happy and secure future: *You must learn how to pick your allies.*

Picking Your Allies

You have seen how to improve your survival chances through better health and a more sensible life-style. You have seen how such factors as attitude and personal preparedness can make the difference between survival and failure—in the future as well as in the present. And we have talked about changing to a simpler life-style that can minimize many of the risks you face in today's complicated, challenging world.

If you have begun to put some of these ideas into practice you probably already feel better physically and have greater confidence in your future. Feeling better about yourself, you may at this point be tempted to relax or to think you can now handle *anything* the future hands you. Don't! That would be the most dangerous mistake you could possibly make. For everything that we have suggested thus far is still insufficient to save you in the troubled times that lie ahead. Nothing you can do will ensure your survival unless you also move on to Step Four: to survive in tomorrow's world, you will need the most powerful allies you can find.

Ahead of you lies the most awesome time of trouble that this world will ever have seen. Nothing out of the past begins to compare with what humanity will soon be facing. Nearly six hundred years before Christ, the prophet Daniel warned of a far-distant future in which "there will be a time of distress such as has not happened from the beginning of nations until then." Daniel 12:1, NIV. He referred to this period as "the time of the end." Verse 9.

Christ Himself echoed Daniel's warnings: "Portents will appear in sun, moon, and stars. On earth nations will stand helpless, not knowing which way to turn . . . ; men will faint with terror at the thought of all that is coming upon the world." Luke 21:25, NEB.

Evidently some great final catastrophe awaits the world, and repeatedly Bible writers have foreseen it and warned people to prepare. What makes their predictions more fascinating is that several have already come true, centuries after they were given. In Matthew, Luke, and Revelation repeated statements warn of portents appearing in nature—particularly in the sky.

The prophet John, writing in Revelation, tells of a train of supernatural events, happening in a specific order, that will indicate when earth's last crisis is drawing near. "There was a violent earthquake; the sun turned black as a funeral pall and the moon all red as blood; the stars in the sky fell to the earth, like figs shaken down by a gale." Revelation 6:12, 13, NEB. And then, he warned, the next major event would be earth's final time of troubles and the end of human history. Every one of those predictions except the last has already been fulfilled.

In 1755, a massive November earthquake destroyed the city of Lisbon, sending shock waves across Europe, down to the north coast of Africa, and as far west as the New World. Many thousands died. The *Encyclopaedia Britannica* calls it "probably the most famous of all earthquakes.'' Thoughtful people recognized its ominous message as a sign of the approaching end of time.

In succession, the rest of the predictions were fulfilled. In May 1780 the sky over New England turned inexplicably black. Cattle returned to their barns at noon. It was impossible to read without candlelight, and terrified people huddled for hours in what appeared to them to be supernatural darkness. That night the moon rose bloody-red, following perfectly the chronology given by John in Revelation. Again, preachers and poets perceived the larger message.

A few years passed. One November night in 1833, the sky across North America exploded with eerie light as ''more than a billion shooting stars'' fell through the earth's atmosphere, filling the sky with such brilliance that one could read a newspaper in the predawn hours. ''Raining fire,'' one awestruck observer called it, and another pointed out that they all seemed to come from one area in the sky, like a tree being shaken and casting its fruit in every direction. And again, journalists, preachers, and other thought leaders saw it all as a prophetic fulfillment.

Earthquake. Darkness at noon. A strange, bloody moon. And now this—a night when ''the stars fell.'' Everything happened in the exact order given centuries before. In the minds of many people the conclusion was unmistakable—the final events on planet earth were just ahead.

Today millions of people share that conclusion, based on additional evidences we see all around us. ''You must face the fact,'' the apostle Paul wrote. ''The final age of this world is to be a time of troubles. Men will love nothing but money and self; they will be arrogant, boastful, and abusive; with no respect for parents, no gratitude . . . ; implacable in their hatreds, . . . intemperate and fierce." 2 Timothy 3:1-4, NEB.

Elsewhere the Bible warns of "wars and rumours of wars," of "famines . . . and earthquakes in many places." Matthew 24:6, 7. The descriptions are too real to ignore—too correct to explain away. They were given 2000 years ago; yet they read like today's newspaper. Something is coming, and it is time to be getting ready.

But what? Fortunately, that too has been foretold. For millions of people who are too careless to study, it will come as a blinding surprise; for you, that need not happen. For all of us, it is time to look into the future—time to pick the allies that can assure our safety.

First, we'll look at the sort of problems the Bible foretells. Clearly there will be economic chaos. "Come now, you rich, weep and howl for the miseries that are coming upon you. . . . Your gold and silver have rusted. . . . You have laid up treasure for the last days." James 5:1-3, RSV. Or, as another translation so graphically adds, "You have lived on earth in wanton luxury, fattening yourselves like cattle—and the day for slaughter has come." James 5:5, NEB.

Precisely how those events will unfold we can only speculate, but the economy will obviously sink into a crisis that will baffle all efforts by economists or politicians who seek to place business operations back on a secure basis. The economic distress will be world-wide and greater than the colossal financial disasters that have staggered most nations in the last century. Those who have most heavily depended on material possessions apparently will experience great personal suffering.

James's prediction is not difficult to believe, given today's circumstances. Even the calmest government leaders are conceding that the United States, as well as the rest of the world, is "in one devil of a dilemma" and "no man alive has a workable solution." In many countries during the past thirty years, social unrest—the haves versus the have-nots—has already created severe political and economic disruptions that seem to defy solution. James's words have taken on new and stark significance. Other countries seem on the brink. For all countries, it is only a matter of time. Our whole economic-industrial system is based on fragile lines of supply that are becoming as brittle as antique lace. Even the United States now largely depends on other nations for certain materials used in its most sophisticated products—chromium from Zimbabwe and South Africa, aluminum from Jamaica or the Guianas, cobalt from Zaire.

Meanwhile, the world's best currencies are wracked by instability largely caused by the enormous cost of energy. In fact, the welfare of most every nation on earth—rich or poor—hangs from a single thread called petroleum energy. Nothing of any magnitude can happen in an isolated way anymore. When the next big upheaval occurs, it will doubtless be a worldwide affair—and it will be awesome, far surpassing the oil crisis of the mid-1970s.

The Bible also describes the sort of events that are likely to accompany a worldwide financial breakdown, such as social turmoil, multiple wars, and famine. There is even a hint of great destruction coming out of the sky. "There will be great earthquakes, and famines and plagues in many places; in the sky terrors and great portents." "On earth nations will stand helpless, not knowing which way to turn . . . ; men will

faint with terror at the thought of all that is coming
upon the earth; for the celestial powers will be
shaken." Luke 21:11, 25-27, NEB.

Throughout the Bible, in the Old Testament as
well as the New, repeated predictions corroborate
Luke's prophecy. References are made to a colossal,
global fire. "The day of the Lord will come like a
thief, and then the heavens will pass away with a loud
noise, and the elements will be dissolved with fire, and
the earth and the works that are upon it will be burned
up." 2 Peter 3:10, RSV.

No wonder Daniel warned, "There will be a time
of distress such as has not happened from the beginning of nations." Chapter 12:1, NIV. Today we have
technology to bring that prediction to pass, and people
everywhere are wondering how, in the face of such a
future, they can hope to survive.

The answer, of course, is that we can't—not without help. Nothing we have said in the earlier chapters
of this book can possibly prepare you to face the coming ordeal described in Bible prophecy.

But the Bible does more than predict dire times. It
has also provided the survival plan that thousands
have used through the centuries when tough times
overtook them. Although realistically warning that
times will come when "a thousand may fall at your
side, ten thousand close at hand," the Bible also promises survival for those who have picked the right ally in
their times of trouble. Let's go back and read the whole
passage, looking at both the bad news and the good.

You that live in the shelter of the Most High
    and lodge under the shadow of the Almighty,
    who say, 'The Lord is my safe retreat, . . .
A thousand shall fall at your side,

ten thousand close at hand,
but you it shall not touch.

Why? Because you have wisely picked your ally.
Read on:

For you, the Lord is a safe retreat;
    you have made the Most High your refuge.
No disaster shall befall you,
    no calamity shall come upon your home.
                              Psalm 91:1, 2, 7, 9, 10, NEB.

What was the psalmist saying over 3000 years ago?
That there would be times when people would fall by
the thousands. Great destructive forces would sweep
across mankind, to the extent that tens of thousands
would die. *Yet there would be a people who would survive!*

What would be the secret of their survival? Part of
the answer is found in Isaiah 33:

Whole nations shall be heaps of white ash,
    or like thorns cut down and set on fire. . . .
Can any of us live with a devouring fire?
Can any live in endless burning?
The man who lives an upright life and
    speaks the truth,
who scorns to enrich himself by extortion,
who snaps his fingers at a bribe,
who stops his ears to hear nothing of bloodshed,
who closes his eyes to the sight of evil—
that is the man who shall dwell on the heights,
his refuge a fastness in the cliffs,
his bread secure and his water never failing.''
                              Verses 12-16, NEB.

During the overwhelming global chaos soon to be brought on by human self-interest, only those who have come to terms with God can hope to survive. Their security is described in Bible prophecy in the strongest possible terms. They are compared, for example, with men and women protected by granite, with all their basic necessities supplied by a caring God with whom they are at peace. By combining faith and human resourcefulness, they have picked the right Ally.

"Grant us help against the enemy," David prayed, "For deliverance by man is a vain hope." Psalm 60:11, NEB. If we expect to endure on the basis of human advice and alliances, we will be in great danger, for no one on earth has a human answer for the problems faced in the last quarter of the twentieth century. The help we need is supernatural, as the psalmist says clearly: "With God's help we shall do valiantly." Psalm 60:12, NEB. "Because his love is set on me I [God] will deliver him; I will lift him beyond danger, for he knows me by my name. When he calls upon me, I will answer; I will be with him in time of trouble; I will rescue him and bring him to honour." Psalm 91:14, 15, NEB.

In the first century of the Christian era, Paul echoed the psalmist, for he had found such words to be true in his own experience: "My God will supply every need of yours according to his riches in glory in Christ Jesus." Philippians 4:19, RSV.

The final and most important question for your survival plan, therefore, is this: *how do you make God your ally?*

For every complex question we have posed so far in this book, we have given easily followed answers. Fortunately, this one is no exception. Many in the past have followed several simple steps in getting to know God better. In taking these simple steps you will be making God a part of your own survival plan. The first involves an old-fashioned word that we have already used—a word often misunderstood. That word is *faith*.

Let's go back to the story of Abraham, whom we talked about in the last chapter. At a time when most middle-aged men feel settled and resistant to change, God impressed him to leave all that was familiar and safe—family, friends, and financial security in the rich trading oasis of Haran.

To all appearances, the move was illogical. He was leaving familiar surroundings and a secure future for something relatively unknown. Nevertheless, he went. In other words, he traded his human view of the future for God's broader view, even though at the time the move seemed to make little sense. The result? The beginning of the great Jewish nation and the establishment of their homeland. All the result of one man's faith.

The early Christians held Abraham in highest esteem. His life of faith provided a rich model for all who sought God's blessing. Observe what they thought about Abraham's move to Canaan: "By faith Abraham obeyed the call to go out to a land destined for himself and his heirs, and left home without knowing where he was to go. By faith he settled as an alien in the land promised him, living in tents, as did Isaac and Jacob, who were heirs to the same promise. For he was looking forward to the city with firm foundations, whose architect and builder is God." Hebrews 11:8-10, NEB.

Over and over the Bible recounts stories like that, of men and women who realized God had something better for them beyond their own limited horizons—and who submitted in faith to His guidance. Noah, for instance—who endured ridicule for 120 years while building a great ship. All the while he listened to his neighbors jeer and to scientists calling him crazy because rain was impossible—up to the moment the rain began to fall.

Moses was destined to be the next pharaoh of Egypt. But "by faith Moses . . . refused to be called the son of Pharaoh's daughter, preferring to suffer hardship with the people of God rather than enjoy the transient pleasures of sin. He considered the stigma that rests on God's Anointed greater wealth than the treasures of Egypt, for his eyes were fixed upon the coming day of recompense." Hebrews 11:24-26, NEB.

Almost every child knows about brave Daniel, the Jewish prime minister of Persia, who prayed openly and without embarrassment, even though he knew it could cost him his life in a den of famished lions.

The Bible is filled with fascinating stories that tell us about the power of faith. So too are the pages of history since Bible times. Perhaps every day somewhere in the world someone is repeating Abraham's experience, or Daniel's. Concentration-camp horrors, prisoner-of-war experiences, as well as the courage of some neighbor in the face of great and prolonged distress—all have tested the spirit of men and women. Faith, we discover, is the greatest survival tool in all the world.

What is faith? It is a belief so strong that you are willing to trust your life to it. Think about it and you will realize that you exercise faith every day. A traffic light turns green, and you accelerate through the intersection. You board an airplane, see a man in the cockpit with gold stripes on his sleeves, and you have confidence that he can safely guide you seven miles high and put you down at your destination thousands of miles away. You believe in something, and you act on that belief. You have exercised faith.

Why not do the same with God? In this book we have been referring to those who, without seeing God, nonetheless saw all around them the evidences of His existence. They trusted Him to guide them properly, and they followed His advice even when they could not always understand it immediately. The Bible abounds with such stories; and, if you read them with an open mind, you cannot help developing a greater faith in God.

Faith—belief that acts. The most important step of all in your survival plan is to believe in a loving heavenly Father-God, who made the world and who sustains your life. All around we see much evidence of goodness and order: springtime's sunlight awakening new life in trees and bulbs, the birth of a child, the incredibly reliable movement of the stars. In addition to these loving touches of a thoughtful Creator, we see indications without number that God loves the beautiful. Think of the Sterling Silver rose or the meadowlark or a day-old calf. Faith acts because it believes all this about our heavenly Father to be true.

But like a dark shadow, other indications point to a great struggle between beauty and ugliness, right and wrong, order and confusion, life and death. Disease. Polluted skies. Neighborhoods unsafe after dark. Illicit drugs. Drunk drivers and highway fatalities. Assassinations. All evidences of a great conflict as old as history and as current as the nightly news. All the relentless malignity of evil now shaping human affairs for earth's last showdown. These emerging danger signals alarm your neighbors and spark the sale of weapons and survival literature. Nearly everyone senses in one way or another that some final confrontation is about to begin.

That is why faith is so important to you. If you believe that a caring God wants to help you, faith can summon to your aid all the power of divine guidance and protection. The Bible is full of promises proved valid by others. Men and women of faith do not fear the future. Neither should you. God is able to intervene in your life when you ask Him. And you can ask Him for His wisdom and strength right now. Perhaps more than all else, He offers His outstretched hand of peace to all those repenting hearts who want His forgiveness. Simply believe that His promises are for you. "For God so loved the world that he gave his only Son, that whoever believes [has faith] in him should not perish but have eternal life." John 3:16, RSV. That sounds like a tremendous survival plan to us!

None of us has any idea of all that will happen when we offer God our faith in response to His offer of pardon and power. Perhaps you have noticed that most of our survival suggestions also have a side benefit—a spin-off—into your present life. You prepare for the future by being healthy today. You prepare by becoming more adaptable and useful—and your career today benefits. You become a man or woman of faith—and your whole life expands to new dimensions. Why? Because of the Person in whom your faith rests.

Twenty centuries ago a man was born amid the most unpromising circumstances, facing all the survival challenges you could imagine. His nation was occupied by foreign armies. Troops were visible everywhere. His parents were poor. He was born in a stable—the only lodging His parents could find on the night of His birth. Soon after He was born, a corrupt government tried to take His life by killing all male babies His age; only by a miracle did He escape. For thirty years he worked as a carpenter in a city notorious for its crime. And then one day He began to preach.

He spoke as no man had ever spoken—not pompous sermons, but simple stories out of the world of nature that quickly fixed the deepest subjects in the minds of young and old, learned and common alike. Man, He said, was like a vine, connected by faith to a loving God. Truth, He likened to seed sown in human minds. Security, He compared to God's care for the lilies and the birds. They never struggle with the commodities market, never worry about the threats of tomorrow, yet they survive because of God's sustaining power. And He reminded people that even sadness does not escape God's notice. Even the death of a little brown sparrow does not pass unnoticed at the throne of heaven; how much more God cares about His sons and daughters whom He made in His own image.

He could talk like that about God because He was God—a mysterious combination of humanity and divinity that brought heaven into human form and showed mankind once and for all what their heavenly Father was really like. At the same time, He was also showing men and women what it meant to be truly human—what they could be like after His restoring touch.

Yet, in becoming human, He subjected Himself to all the risks common to humanity. He entered a hostile world where the forces of evil were deeply entrenched, where His unselfish life brought angry reactions from men and women who did not care to be reminded of their own greediness. One day, enraged at His faultless integrity and kindness, they killed Him by nailing Him to a cross just outside Jerusalem.

Strange as it seems, to face death was one of the reasons He had become man. Imagine Christ, the Creator, willingly facing this terrifying human uncertainty. No play-acting here. Without flinching, without losing His faith, with no more reason to hope than is available to any other person with faith, He followed humanity into the dark valley. He showed us how to die even as He was offering Himself in behalf of all sinners—even those who were murdering Him. He died that repentant sinners might live forever. He is our Saviour.

But God had more on His mind than to show us how to die heroically. On that Sunday morning He showed the universe who holds the key to the grave. With the same creative power that had once fashioned a blue-white world, He brought light even through the gates of death. The Bible account says simply that on the third day after His crucifixion, Christ rose again—and from His open tomb the light of eternity once again flooded the world, as free as sunlight for anyone who cared to use that priceless key called *faith*.

Why is faith important for your survival? Because it holds the key to something even stronger than death. It is your first step in knowing God. "This is eternal life, that they know thee the only true God, and Jesus Christ whom thou hast sent." John 17:3, RSV.

Get to know Him well. All around you are evidences of His goodness: the marvels of migrating birds and fish, the seed that matures as promised, the intricacies of the human body. Look for Him in everything that is beautiful, in anything that reminds you of how life endures in the worst of circumstances. The eye of faith will find Him as close as the simplest flower. And you will find His hand at the limits of man's reach, where our most sensitive telescopes pull in upwards of twelve billion light-years of space.

But you don't have to use a microscope or a telescope to find God at work. Look for Him in the little acts of kindness that still grace our world—in the compassion and faithfulness of those who have responded to His Spirit. Unselfish, caring service to others is one of the best evidences that God has found a home in that person's life.

He can also be found as we read our Bibles. He has not left us in a perplexing world without advice on how to live or what to expect in the future. More than merely fascinating reading, the Bible is a human survival manual, filled with practical advice on health, diet, human nature, and how to get ready to meet Christ at death or at His glorious return. Furthermore, it tells of events just ahead and explains what we can do to prepare for the future. Simply put, the Bible is God's open letter to us—His way of introducing Himself and of telling how He plans to help us in sunshine or shadow. Even more clearly than nature, the Bible reveals God to men and women of faith—the God who once made us and who promises to save us from the penalty and consequences of this awful mess called sin.

Now it is time to end our book on the happiest of all notes. Soon—very soon, it seems—you will see Him. All the signs in nature, in history, and in human behavior combine to say that the end of history as we know it cannot be far away. Just before Christ returns to this earth, a time of trouble will shake civilization to its foundations. It will be a time when many will suffer needlessly, simply because they did not trust in God. They thought instead that they could face the future unassisted. You need not be found in that group.

One of the last-day problems will be great confusion and trouble over religious truth. As the crisis heats up, men and women everywhere will begin to realize that it is, ultimately, a religious issue that troubles the world. More than economics, more than the "right" neighborhood, more than education, human survival itself will seem to be at stake.

Out of this confusion, when all that was ever secure unravels, a great pressure will develop to create worldwide religious unity for the sake of mankind's survival. Perhaps even the power of national legislation will be called upon to enforce religious practices. When that happens, the world will see unimaginable confusion and trouble. Friend will turn on friend, and families will divide—just as every past effort to force the conscience of others has resulted in injustice and suffering.

John the revelator predicted that the day would come at the end of time when those who refuse to comply with the prevailing majority would have great difficulty in even finding food because "no one can buy or sell unless he has the mark." In fact, those who persist in their noncompliance were "to be slain." Revelation 13:16, 17, 15, RSV. Again the world will see death decrees because of religious issues!

Force is a weapon God never employs. He seeks to draw men by demonstrations of His goodness. He never drives them, never overwhelms a person's privilege to choose. Yet force is a weapon frequently used in His name by those who want others to conform to their viewpoint. In a crisis, people tend to look for the "man on the white horse" who will suddenly solve all their problems. In doing so, often willingly, they sacrifice their liberty in the hope that raw power and enforced unity will ensure their survival—forgetting that liberty and survival are synonymous, that the latter is meaningless without the former.

"Give me liberty, or give me death," Patrick Henry is reported to have said, as a new nation was being formed on the platform of civil and religious freedom. That call to freedom seems even more urgent today.

As the earth's last great struggle deepens to involve religious oppression, you will—if you have carefully studied the Bible and acted on its truths—find yourself in a dwindling minority. John calls this group "the remnant," and he describes how cosmic forces will join with earthly powers "to make war with the remnant of her seed, which keep the commandments of God, and have the testimony of Jesus Christ." Revelation 12:17.

At that time the majority will be reciting what appear to be Bible truths; few will be *living* them. Paul saw that too: "You must face the fact: the final age of this world is to be a time of troubles. Men will love nothing but money and self. . . . They will be men who put pleasure in the place of God, men who preserve the outward form of religion, but are a standing denial of its reality." "For the time will come when they will not stand wholesome teaching, but will follow their own fancy and gather a crowd of teachers to tickle their ears. They will stop their ears to the truth and turn to mythology." 2 Timothy 3:1-5; 4:3, 4, NEB.

But God gives us a simple test by which His followers will be distinguished from the great majority who profess religious truth while demonstrating their lack of it as they attempt to force the consciences of their neighbors. That description is found in the amazing fourteenth chapter of Revelation—a chapter that reveals what this world will hear during those last hours, while its evening sun sets on earthly hopes. John the revelator reveals God's last appeal, expressed in three distinct parts and closing with three distinguishing marks that identify His waiting people: "Here is a call for the endurance of the saints, those who keep the commandments of God and the faith of Jesus.'' Revelation 14:12, RSV.

God's people will have learned how to endure, especially during tough times; they will have learned the joy and peace of keeping God's commandments through the grace and strength He gives them. They will have learned how to face life's challenges with the same kind of faith that made Jesus resilient and unafraid.

Obviously, this set of requirements is not new. Men and women of faith have known of no other way to meet life's challenges successfully. They have learned to say Yes to God regardless of earthly circumstances, discovering that happy obedience to His will was their key to peace and to personality fulfillment.

This latter-day test of keeping the commandments of God flows out of the dawn of human history. It rests on one of the oldest documents known to man—a set of ten rules we have come to call the Ten Commandments.

Nearly everyone in all lands is aware of that set of principles. Many of the ideas in the Ten Commandments have been incorporated into every country's civil laws. Do not steal. Do not lie. Respect and care for parents. Respect marriage. In fact, nine out of the ten are so evidently necessary for an orderly society that few people would argue with them. Only one of those ten principles seems to be different from the others. All the rest make sense from a human point of view. This one does not. It is arbitrary. For it to make any sense at all, one has to have absolute faith that God exists and that His Word is the safest, wisest guide for life itself. Which commandment are we talking about? The fourth—the one that establishes a day of rest and worship.

At the end of creation week, with a "good" world before Him and humanity's parents at His side, the Creator rested; not a rest born of weariness but a moment of supreme satisfaction—of reflection on the beautiful truths He had woven into a world of life. In a small way, mankind would know such moments: the warmth of a new life in a mother's arms, the crunch of lunar soil, the creation of a powerful symphony. But this seventh day was God's moment, a special part of Himself that He shared with mankind. Evidently it meant a great deal to Him. "So God blessed the seventh day and hallowed it, because on it God rested from all his work which he had done in creation." Genesis 2:3, RSV.

For a long time, human beings remembered Him on that special day—the seventh day of each week. As sunset darkened the western sky on Friday evening, they worshiped Him by laying aside their personal cares and occupations—a continuing memory of that first Sabbath in Eden—a continual reminder that life was a gift from God.

Later God reminded mankind of that day of rest. *"Remember* the sabbath day, to keep it holy," He said to His people as under Moses' leadership they left Egyptian bondage. Over and over the significance of that day turns up in the Bible story. The Old Testament prophets speak of its special, twofold meaning, both as a reminder that God made this earth in seven days and sanctified the seventh as its weekly Sabbath, and as a sign of His creative power in human lives. Every seventh day we are reminded of this promise that all of us can, through His help, be happy, unselfish members of His family. See Ezekiel 20:12, 20, RSV.

Jesus Himself faithfully observed the weekly Sabbath (Luke 4:16) and declared, "The sabbath was made for man, not man for the sabbath; so the Son of man is lord even of the sabbath." Mark 2:27, 28, RSV.

The New Testament apostles, such as Paul, worshiped on the Sabbath, sometimes in a formal church and sometimes in nature, by the banks of a river "where prayer was wont to be made." Acts 16:13. And in Isaiah, the prophetic promise is given that in God's new world, "week by week on the sabbath, all mankind shall come to bow down before me." Isaiah 66:23, NEB.

The Sabbath—a day we have known for centuries as Saturday in the English language and as *Sábado* in Spanish. The day between Good Friday and Easter Sunday. Luke 23:54-56 and 24:1. One encounters it in the very morning of Creation and again shortly following the Exodus. It is reaffirmed at Sinai and repeated throughout the Old Testament as well as in the life of Christ and in the early Christian church. Ultimately, we are told, it will still be observed in that new world that lasts forever.

Yet there is something about this requirement that makes it very different from the other Ten Commandments. Unlike the remaining nine, its particular demand regarding the *seventh* day makes no sense unless you know and trust God without reservation—trust Him enough to give Him a specific part of your week.

The seventh day. Why Saturday? Why not Friday? Or Sunday? Why not *any* day in seven? What is so special about a day? Those are good questions, and they can be answered when one listens to God speak through His prophets in the Bible. Acting upon this information is the experience that the Bible calls faith—that simple word with which we began this discussion of how to know God.

Faith, you will recall, is belief at the point of action. That is, you believe in something or someone enough to *act*. So it is with this special commandment. It stands out from the rest because it requires you to follow God in a particular way, even though your human perspective might see no particular reason for doing so.

In acting by faith you take the same step that Abraham took when, in response to God's call, he did something *simply because God said so*. All the great men and women of faith in all ages have lived this way. Having placed such absolute trust in God, they were able to survive when others could not. They had picked an Ally they could trust absolutely—whether it involved a day of worship, help with their family problems, or moral strength in times of decision making.

And *that* will be the great issue at the end of this world's turbulent history. In a time of great economic stress, when society itself seems to be breaking up, millions the world over, claiming to know God and hoping for His divine intervention, will want to enforce their views on everyone else. But having failed to trust Him in something that seems small to them—the honoring of His day of worship—they will also fail to trust Him with the great issue of their own survival. And they will be needlessly lost in the process.

Remember, God is not holding back secrets. Through John the revelator He has spelled out the difference between the survivors and those who are victims in earth's last terrifying time of trouble. On one hand are those "who keep the commandments of God and the faith of Jesus." Revelation 14:12, RSV. On the other, each one who "worships the beast and its image . . . receives a mark on his forehead or on his hand." Revelation 14:9, RSV. Jesus described those in this latter group as "everyone who hears these words of mine and *does them not.*" Matthew 7:26, RSV.

God's primary concern for men and women everywhere is that they should be survivors. His gospel is a formula for survival. To do things His way is to choose survival. That is why John links love and faith and obedience to God's commandments in an inseparable bond: "This is the love of God, that we keep his commandments. And his commandments are not burdensome. For . . . this is the victory that overcomes the world, our faith." 1 John 5:3, 4, RSV.

Jesus put this matter of survival in another way: "Not everyone who calls me 'Lord, Lord' will enter the kingdom of Heaven, but only those who do the will of my heavenly Father. . . . What then of the man who hears these words of mine and acts upon them? He is like a man who had the sense to build his house on rock. The rain came down, the floods rose, the wind blew, and beat upon that house; but it did not fall, because its foundations were on rock." Matthew 7:21-25, NEB.

Survival. Those who truly survive will have gone back to the foundations of life. They will have found reality and peace in cooperating with nature and the God behind nature. That is why it is so important for you to know what you should believe and why. And why you should act on your belief. Ahead of us lies a time of great confusion, in which even the brightest and best educated may be easily fooled unless they cheerfully respond to the truths revealed in God's Word—our manual for survival.

You have already made an important beginning. You have discovered that tomorrow is not for the weak—only the fit and the useful survive. You have learned about health, and you know where to continue your research. You have seen how a person's life-style and attitude affect his or her preparedness for the future. You have seen how to secure a divine ally and thus make your survival plan complete.

Now the future is up to you. Use it wisely. Continue to read the Bible and the other books we've suggested in Appendix B for your further study. Build upon the truths you have learned, in order to reduce the risks of disease and financial collapse that will overwhelm many in earth's "time of trouble." Above all, you will realize more and more that God truly cares about you and will stand by your side—and even within you—to guarantee that you will be a survivor!

Relatively few will survive the coming ordeal; you can be one of them. And your reward will be to see the face of God as He says to you, personally, "Well done, good and faithful servant. Welcome home."

That is survival!

Appendix A

1. Dr. Lester Breslow, dean of the School of Public Health at the University of California at Los Angeles, with fellow researchers in the Human Population Laboratory of the California State Department of Public Health, began a study of 7000 adult residents of Alameda County, California, in 1965. Their studies led to the conclusion that good health habits rather than a person's initial health status were responsible for the remarkable extension of life expectancy enjoyed by those practicing these habits. Those seven good health habits have been reviewed in chapter 2.

Dr. Breslow has checked and rechecked his statistics, and the results are always the same. He believes that the future of medicine lies in the prevention of disease, not just in its treatment. Among numerous references to the Breslow studies, the reader will enjoy reading an article by Breslow and James E. Enstrom, entitled "Persistence of Health Habits and Their Relationship to Mortality," that appeared in *Preventive Medicine* 9, 469-483 (1980).

2. Frank S. Lemon, M.D., of the University of Kentucky, and Richard Walden, M.D., of Loma Linda University's School of Health, conducted long-term studies of 50,000 California Seventh-day Adventists, comparing the dramatic differences between Adventists' morbidity and mortality rates with the general population. Some of their results are reported in chapter 2. The reader is referred to the following documents for a fuller discussion:

Frank R. Lemon, M.D., and Richard T. Walden, M.D., "Death From Cancer Among Seventh-day Adventists," *Review and Herald,* July 9, 1964.

Frank R. Lemon, M.D., and Richard T. Walden, M.D., "Death From Respiratory System Disease Among Seventh-day Adventist Men," *Journal of the American Medical Association,* vol. 198, no. 2, Oct. 10, 1966.

Ernest L. Wynder, M.D., Frank R. Lemon, M.D., and Irwin J. Bross, Ph.D., "Cancer and Coronary Artery Disease Among Seventh-day Adventists," *Cancer,* vol. 12, no. 5, September-October, 1959.

Appendix B

Other Books You May Enjoy

Health

Diet Without Danger, by Donald W. Hewitt, M.D. 160 pages

A sensible weight-loss or weight-maintenance program written by a physician who has seen firsthand the dangers of fad diets, crash diets, high-protein diets, and high-caloric diets. Published by Pacific Press Publishing Association, Mountain View, California 94042.

How You Can Live Six Extra Years, by Lewis R. Walton, J.D.; Jo Ellen Walton, M.D.; and John A. Scharffenberg, M.D. 128 pages

Simple proven steps that can add six or more years to one's life-span besides enriching the years with good health and happiness. Published by Woodbridge Press Publishing Company, Santa Barbara, California 93111.

It's Your World Vegetarian Cookbook, by Fern Calkins. 304 pages

A remarkable collection of scientific support for vegetarian cookery with more than 500 recipes utilizing natural foods prepared with a minimum of fat, sugar, and dairy products. Published by the Review and Herald Publishing Association, Washington, D.C. 20012.

New Frontiers in Good Health, by Richard Utt. 32 pages

A fresh overview of what has been learned in the recent past regarding how disease can be prevented—and even predicted. Published by Pacific Press.

Lady, I'm Tired Too, by George Vandeman. 64 pages

Written by the internationally known TV speaker for

the "It Is Written" program. The reader will gain a varied program for improving mental and emotional health. Published by Pacific Press.

Oats, Peas, Beans & Barley Cookbook, by Edyth Young Cottrell. 268 pages

A complete vegetarian cookbook from a Loma Linda University research nutritionist. Published by Woodbridge Press.

Thin From Within, by Jack D. Osman, Ph.D. 160 pages

The author, a professor of health science, takes a values-clarification approach to dieting, which is an action program of weight loss. Published by Review and Herald.

375 Meatless Recipes: Century 21 Cookbook, by Ethel R. Nelson, M.D. 164 pages

For those who look for new and exciting ways to prepare the family meal. Published by Eusey Press, 27 Nashua, Leominster, Massachusetts 01453.

General

Abandon Earth: Last Call, by Roy Allan Anderson, D.D. 64 pages

A long-time educator and religious author reviews world conditions in the light of Bible prophecy. Published by Pacific Press.

Because of You, by Lewis R. Walton, J.D. 32 pages

An especially attractive illustrated story of the good news found in the Bible and how God wants to enrich our life today. Published by Pacific Press.

God Cares, by C. Mervyn Maxwell, Ph.D. 320 pages

Perhaps no book in the last one hundred years has done more to unfold the message of the prophet Daniel and its meaning for those in the twentieth century. While faithful to biblical meaning and historical fulfillment, the author's emphasis is to show how God cares for earth's family in all circumstances, sunshine or shadow. Published by Pacific Press.

The End, by Herbert E. Douglass, Th.D. 192 pages

The author sorts out the many voices proclaiming how the world will end and outlines a series of events that will yet transpire before Jesus returns. Published by Pacific Press.

Marked, by Bob Spangler. 158 pages

Amidst the wild speculations concerning "the mark of the beast," the author focuses on what God's Word has said about the "beast" and its "mark"—a clear, beautiful picture of God's plan for your salvation. Published by the Review and Herald.

Parable of the Hurricane, by Herbert E. Douglass, Th.D. 32 pages

The author compares those in the paths of recent hurricanes Camille and David who ignored urgent warnings, with the inexplicable response of many today who are rejecting the signals indicating the storm of trouble just preceding the return of Jesus. Published by Pacific Press.

The Way Out Is Up, by J. O. Wilson. 64 pages

With biblical and historical evidence, the author points to those characteristics that identify the people whom the Bible calls "the remnant" and the exciting future ready for them when Jesus returns. Published by Pacific Press.

Thoughts in Springtime, by Lewis R. Walton, J.D. 32 pages

Using a format similar to *Because of You,* the author writes of the reasons for hope that come to those who treasure the good news of the Bible—the pictures tell the story as much as the words. Published by Pacific Press.

Something for you . . .

☐ Send me a free copy of *Signs of the Times*, the international prophetic monthly.

☐ Enroll me in one of your free Bible courses.

☐ I want information about the Five-Day Plan to Stop Smoking.

☐ I would like more information about the Bible prophecies of Daniel and Revelation.

☐ Send me the address of the nearest Adventist Church.

Complete this coupon below, and mail to

Pacific Press Publishing Association
P.O. Box 7000, Mountain View, CA 94039

_____
Name

_____
Street or Box

_____
City   State   Zip   S